111 Ultimate Ice Cream Recipes

(111 Ultimate Ice Cream Recipes - Volume 1)

Nancy Reed

Content

111 Awesome Ice Cream Recipes

***

1. Café Glacee (Coffee And Vanilla Ice Cream Cocktail)

Serving: Serves 12 or more | Prep: | Cook: | Ready in:

Ingredients

- • 10 cups water
- • 20 teaspoons the best quality coffee
- • ½ a cup sugar
- • ¼ cup coffee liquor
- • ¼ cup vanilla cream liquor
- • 1pint of coffee ice cream
- • 1pint vanilla bean ice cream

Direction

- In a large pot bring water, coffee and sugar to a boil. Take of the stove, cool to room temperature, strain thru a fine sift to a beautiful large glass pitcher. Cover and transfer to refrigerator to chill. When ready to serve, remove from refrigerator, and mix in the liquors.
- At the table pour the chilled coffee to tall wine glasses. Fill the glasses 2/3 of the way. Ask your guests to choose their favorite ice cream or both, and add a scoop or two to the glass.
- Enjoy!!!

2. Pecan Brittle Ice Cream

Serving: Makes 1 quart | Prep: | Cook: | Ready in:

Ingredients

- Almond Cream and quick and easy brittle
- 3 1/2 cups raw almonds
- 3 cups filtered or spring water
- pinch of salt
- Quick Pecan Brittle
- 2 tablespoons dairy free butter
- 1/2 cup loose brown sugar (dark or light)
- 2-3 tablespoons dark corn syrup or golden syrup (for a harder candy use 2 and softer use 3)
- 1/2-3/4 cups pecans broken into pieces (depending on how many nuts you like)
- generous pinch of sea salt
- Custard base and Making the ice cream
- 3 cups almond cream
- 1/2 cup sugar
- pinch salt
- 1 teaspoon corn starch
- 1 tablespoon vanilla extract

Direction

- Almond Cream and quick and easy brittle
- Soak almonds overnight in spring or filtered water. Drain almonds after soaking, place in food processor with 3 cups water, salt and process. Strain through nut bag, cheese cloth or sieve. Refrigerate until ready to use.
- I did not use a candy thermometer for the brittle, melt the butter in a small saucepan add the brown sugar and cook until the sugar is completely melted and its smooth, add the syrup and salt and pecans and cook on medium an additional five minutes stirring continuously. Line a small sheet pan with parchment or silpat and scrape the brittle onto it, spread as best you can, I pressed it flat with a doubled piece of parchment paper. Allow to cool, it will get pretty hard, break into pieces and chop it into small fine pieces. Place in lidded container and store until ready to use. Cooking the brown sugar mixture the full 5 minutes yields a fairly hard candy, it's kind of

a cross between toffee and a brittle. It works beautifully in the ice cream.

- Custard base and Making the ice cream
- Add all the ingredients except for the vanilla into a heavy saucepan. Heat on medium high whisking constantly until custard becomes thickened and coats the back of the spoon. Remove from heat, add the vanilla. Pour into a heat proof container, cover with plastic wrap directly on the custard. Bring to room temperature and refrigerate overnight.
- Make the ice cream according to manufacturer's directions on your ice cream maker. When it's sufficiently thick add the crushed/finely chopped brittle. Spoon into freezer container and freeze until it's scoopable consistency.

3. AUNT JANET'S SPA MOJITO

Serving: Serves 1-2 | Prep: | Cook: |Ready in:

Ingredients

- For Lemonade:
- 3/4 cup organic cane sugar
- 1 cup water
- 1 cup fresh squeezed lemon juice, seeds and pulp strained
- 2 cups ice
- For Frozen Mojito:
- 1/2 cup ice
- 1/2 cup lemonade (recipe above)
- 4   fresh mint leaves
- 1 1/2 -2 ounces good light rum

Direction

- MAKE LEMONADE: In a small saucepan, heat the water and sugar over MEDIUM heat. Stir constantly until sugar is dissolved, about 5 minutes. Pour into a pitcher. Add lemon juice and stir to combine. Add water and ice. Adjust the amount of water to your taste if you like.

Refrigerate until chilled, 30 minutes. Taste and add more lemon juice if it is too sweet.

- MAKE THE FROZEN MINT MOJITO: In a blender, combine 1/2 cup of the chilled lemonade. Add mint leaves, and rum. Blend. Garnish your glass with a sprig of mint and enjoy.

4. Ada Boni's Fresh Strawberry Granita Or Sorbet

Serving: Serves about 6 | Prep: | Cook: |Ready in:

Ingredients

- 8 ounces (200 grams/1 quart) strawberries
- 1/2 cup lemon juice (about 2 lemons)
- 1/4 cup orange juice (about 1 orange)
- 2 1/2 cups (750 ml) water
- 2 1/2 cups (500 grams) granulated sugar

Direction

- Make a simple syrup by combining the water and sugar in a saucepan. Bring to a boil and let simmer 10 minutes. Remove and let cool completely.
- Remove the leaves off the strawberries and blend them in a blender or food processor with the lemon and orange juice. Add the cooled syrup—but note, I recommend tasting as you add it. If you have particularly sweet strawberries or not very sour lemons (like Meyer lemons) you probably will not need all of it. Even just half this amount can still be enough to make it set nicely.
- If making granita, place the strawberry liquid in a shallow, flat baking dish (something like a glass or ceramic lasagna pan would be perfect) so that the liquid is no more than a couple inches deep. If this doesn't fit in your freezer (I recommend measuring first before you put the liquid in), you can use a loaf pan or similar shaped container, just note that it will take significantly longer to freeze this way (those

containers are just fine for making sorbet). Place container in the freezer, and after an hour, "fluff" it with a fork, particularly around the edges, where it will freeze first. Keep doing this every 30 to 60 minutes, until it is an icy "mush," as Ada Boni says. Serve in glasses with a spoon and a straw.

- If making sorbet, simply let it freeze overnight (a deeper pan or container can be used). Let it rest about 10 minutes outside of the freezer and scoop into bowls.

5. Affogato

Serving: Serves 4 | Prep: | Cook: | Ready in:

Ingredients

- 1 pint vanilla gelato or ice cream (the good stuff!)
- 4 long shots espresso

Direction

- Scoop the ice cream into 4 bowls. Pour a shot of espresso over each mound of ice cream. Serve quickly!

6. All Purpose Streusel

Serving: Makes 6 cups | Prep: | Cook: | Ready in:

Ingredients

- 8 ounces unsalted butter
- 2 cups all-purpose flour
- 1/2 cup granulated sugar
- 1/2 cup dark brown sugar
- 1 cup thick-cut rolled oats
- 1 cup cups walnuts, chopped
- 1 teaspoon kosher salt
- 1 teaspoon ground cinnamon

Direction

- Melt the butter and keep warm.
- Combine the rest of the ingredients in a large bowl. Pour in the warm butter and mix until most of the dry ingredients are moistened but it is still clumpy.
- Spread the streusel out onto a baking sheet, keeping it clumpy, and refrigerate for 30 minutes or more to set.
- Top fresh or frozen fruit, a batch of blueberry muffins or bake and top some vanilla ice cream. Freeze in ziploc bags for up to 6 months.

7. Allergies Be Gone! Smoothie

Serving: Serves 2 | Prep: | Cook: | Ready in:

Ingredients

- For the smoothie:
- 1/2 English cucumber, chopped
- 1 bunch bunch flat-leaf parsley, chopped
- 2 medium lemons, peeled and seeded
- 2 cups (320 grams) frozen pineapple
- 5 drops alcohol-free liquid stevia, plus more to taste
- Optional boosters:
- 1 teaspoon wheatgrass powder
- 1 teaspoon minced ginger
- 1/4 cup (30 grams) frozen raw cauliflower florets

Direction

- Throw all of the ingredients into your blender and blast on high for about 1 minute, until smooth and creamy. Tweak sweetener to taste.

8. Almond Ice With Glazed Cherries

Serving: Serves 4 | Prep: | Cook: |Ready in:

Ingredients

- For the ice
- 4 1/4 cups water
- 2 cups almonds (with skins on), chopped
- 1 teaspoon aniseed or fennel seed
- 1/2 teaspoon salt
- 4 1/2 tablespoons sugar
- For the cherries
- 2 1/2 cups cherries
- 2 1/4 cups water
- 3/4 cup dried cherries
- 3 ounces Aperol or Campari (or other bitter aperitif)

Direction

- Bring the water to a boil. In a bowl, combine the almonds, aniseed, salt, and sugar. Pour in the boiling water. Let cool, then refrigerate overnight. (If you don't have time to let it sit overnight, don't worry, just move on to the next step.)
- Puree the almond mixture in a blender and get it as smooth as possible. Strain through cheesecloth into measuring cup with a spout. Pour into ice cube trays and freeze.
- When the almond ice cubes are completely frozen, fit your food processor with the grating blade. Grate the ice cubes, a few at time. Immediately transfer the almond snow to a freezer container and freeze the grated almond ice.
- Meanwhile, make the cherry glaze: pit the cherries, reserving the pits. In a small saucepan, combine 1 1/2 cups fresh cherries, the water, reserved pits, dried cherries, and Aperol. Bring to a simmer and cook gently for 30 minutes. Strain the mixture, pressing the solids to extract as much juice as possible, into a clean saucepan. Boil this mixture until it's a light syrup.
- Just before serving, fold the remaining 1 cup fresh cherries into the syrup. Spoon the almond ice into chilled shallow bowls, making a small well in the center. Spoon a few cherries and some syrup into the well. Enjoy – quickly!

9. Amaretto Affogato

Serving: Serves 1 | Prep: | Cook: |Ready in:

Ingredients

- For Amaretto Ice Cream:
- 6 tablespoons unsalted butter, cut into cubes
- 2 cups 2% milk
- 3 tablespoons brown sugar
- 1/2 vanilla bean, scored down the length with a sharp knife
- 6 large egg yolks
- 4 tablespoons granulated sugar
- 1 cup heavy cream
- 1/4 cup Amaretto liqueur
- +++++++++++++++++++++++
- For Amaretto Affogato:
- 1 scoop Amaretto ice cream
- 1 hot shot of your favorite espresso (I used Stumptown Roasters Hair Bender espresso beans)

Direction

- In a shallow heavy bottomed pan, melt butter over medium heat. Continue to cook butter – it should foam up a bit and then subside – until brown specks begin to form at the bottom. It should have a pleasant, nutty aroma. Remove from heat and set aside.
- In a saucepan, heat milk, brown sugar. Using a sharp knife, scrape vanilla beans into pan; cook mixture, stirring occasionally, to dissolve brown sugar and incorporate vanilla. Remove from heat.
- Beat egg yolks in a large bowl, gradually adding granulated sugar. You want the mixture to be thick and pale.

- Temper the egg mixture by ladling some of the warmed milk into the beaten yolks, whisking constantly.
- Slowly pour tempered egg mixture back into remaining warm milk, whisking constantly, and cook over medium heat until mixture becomes thick. Add browned butter, stirring to combine. Remove from heat.
- Pour heavy cream into a heat proof glass bowl or Pyrex measure. Using a sieve, strain custard into container with cream; stir to combine, add Amaretto, and stir again. Cover container with plastic wrap and transfer to refrigerator. Chill in the coldest part of your refrigerator for at least two hours, nesting the container in a larger bowl with ice cubes and a little water.
- When ready to make ice cream, pour chilled custard into bowl of ice cream maker. Continue to process, following the manufacturer's directions. After 40 minutes, ice cream will still be quite soft. Transfer to a container and freeze for at least a day before using.
- To make affogato, serve one scoop of Amaretto ice cream in coffee cups or bowls of choice. Pour espresso over ice cream and enjoy.

10. America's Test Kitchen's Instant Aged Balsamic Vinegar

Serving: Makes about 1/4 cup | Prep: | Cook: |Ready in:

Ingredients

- 1/3 cup balsamic vinegar
- 1 tablespoon sugar
- 1 tablespoon port

Direction

- Combine ingredients in shallow, nonreactive pan and slowly reduce over extremely low heat. Mixture should be barely simmering. Continue until mixture is reduced to half its original volume. Let cool to room temperature and use immediately.
- Serve over vanilla ice cream or panna cotta, on ripe pears or strawberries, with cheeses (especially, but not limited to, Parmesan), stirred into soups and drizzled over grilled steaks and pork chops—or anywhere else your food could use a hit of bright, sweet tang.

11. Avocado Coconut Ice Cream

Serving: Serves 3 | Prep: | Cook: | Ready in:

Ingredients

- 2 avocado
- 250 milliliters coconut milk
- 125 milliliters coconut cream
- 100 grams sugar
- 1 teaspoon lime juice
- 1 teaspoon rum
- 1 pinch salt

Direction

- Combine all the ingredients in a blender and whizz away until glossy and smooth (and velvety and yummy already). (The avocados should be ripe, but firm, pits and skins removed).
- Transfer the mixture into a jug and refrigerate overnight. Freeze in your ice cream maker according to manufacturer's instructions. Store in an airtight container in the freezer for at least 4 hours until set or spoon right away.

12. Baklava Ice Cream

Serving: Makes about 1 quart | Prep: | Cook: |Ready in:

Ingredients

- Ice cream base

- 2 cups whole milk
- 1 tablespoon 1 teaspoon cornstarch
- 3 tablespoons cream cheese, at room temperature
- 1/8 teaspoon fine sea salt
- 3 cinnamon sticks
- 1/2 cup honey
- 1 cup shelled walnuts, chopped
- 24 pre-made frozen mini phyllo shells
- Rose-water syrup
- 1/2 cup sugar
- 1/3 cup water
- 1 tablespoon rose water

Direction

- In a small bowl, stir together 1/4 cup of the milk and the cornstarch and set aside.
- In a large bowl, whisk the cream cheese and salt together, and set aside.
- Combine the remaining milk, the cream, the split vanilla beans, and the cinnamon sticks in a 4-quart saucepan, bring to a low, rolling boil, and cook for four minutes.
- Remove the mixture from the heat, stir in the cornstarch mixture and the honey.
- Return the mixture to a boil, and cook, stirring, until the mixture is slightly thickened, for one or two minutes (note: if it doesn't thicken much, don't worry).
- Gradually whisk the hot milk/cream mixture into the cream cheese.
- Chill the mixture overnight (or use Jeni's quick-cool method).
- Make the syrup by combining the sugar and water and bringing to a boil to dissolve the sugar. Add the rose water, return to a boil, cook for 3-4 minutes, and then let cool.
- Remove the vanilla beans and cinnamon sticks from the chilled base.
- Freeze the ice cream according to your ice cream maker's instructions.
- In a freezer-safe container, add a layer of the ice cream base, then drizzle in a layer of syrup, then add a layer of chopped nuts, then another layer of ice cream, and so on, until the container is full.

- Cover with a sheet of parchment cut to size, seal container tightly, and freeze for several hours until hard.
- To serve, warm the phyllo shells according to package directions. Use a teaspoon or small cookie or ice cream scoop to make a tiny scoop of ice cream and place it in the crisped shell. If you have any syrup or nuts left, you can add a final drizzle or sprinkle to the top of the ice cream. Serve 2-3 mini scoops/shells per person.

13. Balsamic Strawberry Ice Cream And Dark Chocolate Cookie Sandwiches

Serving: Makes at least 10 sandwiches | Prep: | Cook: | Ready in:

Ingredients

- Balsamic Strawberry Ice Cream
- 1 1/2 pints strawberries, preferably organic, hulled and halved or quartered
- 2 1/2 tablespoons sugar
- 2 teaspoons balsamic vinegar
- 5 large egg yolks
- 1/2 cup sugar
- 1 3/4 cups heavy cream
- 3/4 cup 1% or 2% milk
- 1/4 teaspoon kosher salt
- 2 teaspoons balsamic vinegar
- Dark Chocolate Cookies
- 2 2/3 cups unbleached ?all-purpose flour
- 2 cups Dutch-processed cocoa powder, measured then sifted
- 4 1/2 teaspoons baking soda
- 1/2 teaspoon kosher salt
- 15 ounces unsalted butter, at room temperature
- 2 cups granulated sugar
- 1 cup packed light or dark brown sugar
- 3 large eggs

Direction

- Balsamic Strawberry Ice Cream
- Cook the berries: Combine the berries with the 2 1/2 tablespoons sugar and 2 teaspoons vinegar in a large nonreactive skillet. Put the skillet over medium heat and cook, stirring frequently, until the strawberries are soft and the liquid they release has reduced somewhat, 6 to 8 minutes. Let cool slightly, then transfer the berries and their juice to a blender or food processor. Purée until smooth and refrigerate until ready to use.
- Make the ice cream base: In a medium heatproof bowl, whisk the yolks just to break them up, then whisk in half of sugar (1/4 cup). Set aside.
- In a heavy nonreactive saucepan, stir together the cream, milk, salt, and the remaining sugar (1/4 cup) and put the pan over medium-high heat. When the mixture approaches a bare simmer, reduce the heat to medium.
- Carefully scoop out about 1/2 cup of the hot cream mixture and, whisking the eggs constantly, add the cream to the bowl with the egg yolks. Repeat, adding another 1/2 cup of the hot cream to the bowl with the yolks. Using a heatproof rubber spatula, stir the cream in the saucepan as you slowly pour the egg-and-cream mixture from the bowl into the pan.
- Cook the mixture carefully over medium heat, stirring constantly, until it is thickened, coats the back of a spatula, and holds a clear path when you run your finger across the spatula, 1 to 2 minutes longer.
- Strain the base through a fine-mesh strainer into a clean container. Set the container into an ice-water bath, wash your spatula, and use it to stir the base occasionally until it is cool. Remove from the ice-water bath, cover with plastic wrap, and refrigerate the base for at least 2 hours or overnight.
- Freeze ice cream: Whisk the strawberry purée and the remaining 2 teaspoons vinegar into the chilled base. Freeze in your ice cream machine according to the manufacturer's instructions. While the ice cream is churning, put the container you'll use to store the ice cream into the freezer. Enjoy right away or, for a firmer ice cream, transfer to the chilled container and freeze for at least 4 hours.
- Dark Chocolate Cookies
- In a medium bowl, whisk together the flour, cocoa powder, baking soda, and salt and set aside.
- In the bowl of a stand mixer with the paddle attachment, combine the butter and both sugars. Mix on medium-high speed until lightened in color and fluffy, about 2 minutes. Scrape down the bowl and, with the motor running, add the eggs one at a time, completely mixing in each egg before adding the next.
- Scrape down the sides of the bowl, add the flour mixture, and mix on low speed just until the dough comes together, about 30 seconds.
- Cover the bowl with plastic wrap and chill until the dough is firm, at least 2 hours or up to overnight.
- When you're ready to bake, position racks in the top and bottom thirds of the oven and preheat the oven to 350°F. Line two baking sheets with parchment paper or nonstick mats. Scoop up 2 tablespoons of dough (we use a 1-ounce ice cream scoop) and form the dough into a ball. Repeat until all the dough has been shaped. Place the balls 2 1/2 inches apart on the baking sheets. Flatten the balls slightly with the palm of your hand so that they're about 1/2 inch thick.
- Bake for 5 minutes, and then rotate the baking sheets top to bottom and front to back. Continued to bake until the cookies are slightly cracked on the surface and feel dry and slightly firm in the center, 5 to 6 minutes longer. (If they feel airy, like a soufflé, they're not ready.)Let cool for a minute on the baking sheets, then transfer to a rack. Bake the remaining dough balls. Let cool completely and then store in an airtight container.
- Tip: Sometimes having 50 cookies in your kitchen is more temptation than you want at one time! If that's the case for you, try what we

do when making cookies at home: After mixing the cookie dough, shape the dough into balls and line them up snugly on a parchment paper–lined baking sheet. Freeze until solid (about an hour), then transfer to a zip-top storage bag and store in the freezer. They last for weeks this way, and you can bake as many or as few as you like at a moment's notice. When you're ready to bake, arrange the dough balls on the baking sheet and let them sit at room temperature to thaw slightly before putting them in the oven.

- For ice cream sandwiches: Get the cookies ready, arranging half of them upside down on a baking sheet. You can get a uniform shape by using a dry measuring cup as a mold for the ice cream. Or, you can get a more handmade look by simply scooping a large scoop of ice cream onto a cookie, sandwiching it with a second cookie, and pressing on the cookies slightly. Freeze the sandwiches, putting the baking sheet in the freezer to let them harden for at least two hours. If you're storing the sandwiches for longer than one day, transfer the hardened sandwiches to zip-top freezer bags, being sure to squeeze out any excess air before sealing.

14. Banoffee Pie Ice Cream

Serving: Serves 4 | Prep: | Cook: | Ready in:

Ingredients

- 200 milliliters whole milk
- 380 milliliters heavy cream
- 180 grams sugar
- 1 pinch salt
- 3 teaspoons cornstarch
- 50 grams cream cheese
- 1 large banana
- 45 grams milk chocolate
- 45 grams shortbread fingers

Direction

- For the caramel ripple sprinkle 100gr sugar evenly over the bottom of a heavy-duty 4-quart saucepan, set it over medium high heat and cook barely stirring only when the inner layer of sugar starts to melt, mix the liquified sugar with the crystallized sugar on top of it very gently. Don't overstir. When all of the sugar is liquified continue cooking on low stirring until the caramel is penny-bronze in color. Take off heat, slowly add 180ml heavy cream a little at a time, stirring constantly until fully incorporated. If there are any lumps of sugar left, return on medium heat and stir until completely melted. Take off heat, add a tiny pinch of salt, cool to room temperature and store in a sealed jug until ready to use.
- For the milk chocolate shaves run the knife across the surface of a chocolate bar at room temperature.
- For the shortbread crumbs crush the shortbread cookies into bite size chunks.
- Dissolve 3tsp in 50ml whole milk, leave to rest.
- In a small saucepan over medium heat combine 200ml heavy cream, the leftover milk, 80gr sugar and a pinch of salt, stir, bring to an almost boil, add the cornstarch milk and cook constantly stirring until thickened. Take off heat, add the cream cheese and fresh banana purée, stir until smooth. Cool to room temperature, then transfer into the fridge overnight.
- Freeze in your ice cream maker according to the manufacturer's instructions adding the shortbread pieces and chocolate shaves at the last couple of minutes of churning. Transfer into an airtight container, swirling in pockets of the caramel sauce (use half the amount that you prepared) and store in the freezer for at least 4 hours until firm enough to scoop.

15. Blue Cheese And Peaches Ice Cream

Serving: Serves 2 pints | Prep: | Cook: | Ready in:

Ingredients

- 2 cups Whole milk
- 4 teaspoons Corn starch
- 1 1/2 ounces Blue cheese
- 1/8 teaspoon Fine sea salt
- 1 1/4 cup Heavy Cream
- 2/3 cup Sugar
- 2 tablespoons Light Corn Syrup
- 2 to 3 Peaches, chopped

Direction

- In a small bowl, mix about 2 tablespoons of the milk with the cornstarch to make a smooth slurry. In a medium bowl, add the salt and room-temperature cream cheese and whip all the bumps out. In a large bowl, make an ice bath (heavy on the ice) and set aside.
- Pour the cream, sugar, corn syrup, and remaining milk into a 4-quart saucepan. Bring to a rolling boil over medium-high heat, set a timer for precisely 4 minutes and boil for exactly 4 minutes — the timing is critical. Remove from the heat and gradually whisk in the cornstarch slurry. Return the mixture to a boil over medium-high heat and cook, stirring until the mixture is slightly thickened, about 1 minute. Remove from the heat.
- Gradually whisk the hot milk mixture into the blue cheese until smooth. Do this a little bit at a time so that you can whip out any lumps of blue cheese. Pour the mixture into the ice cream maker and churn it as per your ice-cream maker's instruction manual and once the ice cream is done, remove it and add the chopped peaches and mix it with a spatula.
- Pour the chilled base into the container and seal with an airtight lid. Freeze in the coldest part of your freezer until firm, at least 4 hours.
- When you remove the ice cream from the freezer, let it sit and relax for 5 to 10 minutes before you scoop and serve it — it doesn't need to melt, but it does need to thaw slightly. Ideally, serve and eat it while it's quite firm but pliable and you are able to easily roll it into a ball. Once you've scooped it, return any remaining ice cream to the freezer. If the ice cream has melted too much at room temperature, refreezing it will result in an ice cream that is too icy.
- If you do not want bits or pieces of peaches, you can also make a pulp out of it and mix it right before churning. I like the chopped pieces or bite of peaches so I churned the ice cream first and then added the peaches. Go for whatever you like. There are no hard rules. I have totally adapted Jeni's ice cream recipe, so if there is any confusion then follow her basic recipe sub cream cheese to blue cheese of your choice and add peaches. And, there you have wonderful ice-cream. Garnish it with mint leaves, if you wish to. How I would like to serve it - I would cut very thin triangle slices of blue cheese and place it right next to the ice-cream scoop and top the ice cream with some sliced caramelized peach. Yum!

16. Blueberry Cobbler No Churn Ice Cream

Serving: Makes half a loaf pan | Prep: | Cook: | Ready in:

Ingredients

- No Churn Ice Cream
- 1 1/2 cups condensed milk (full fat)
- 3/4 cup heavy whipping cream
- 1/2 teaspoon vanilla extract
- Blueberry Cobbler Chunks
- 3/4 cup all purpose flour
- 1/4 cup whole wheat pastry flour (or sub with AP flour+1 tbsp)
- 1/2 teaspoon salt
- 2 tablespoons white sugar
- 5 tablespoons super cold unsalted butter
- 1/4 cup milk of choice
- 1/2 teaspoon vanilla extract
- 11 ounces pack of fresh blueberries

Direction

- Start with the cream base. Keep a loaf pan in the freezer until the pan is ready to be filled. Pour all three ice cream ingredients in the order listed into a large bowl and whisk vigorously. Keep whisking until faint trails start to appear in the mixture, but it doesn't need to form stiff peaks or anything close to that. It takes about 4 minutes of whisking. Pour the cream base into the cold loaf pan and freeze for 3 hours. In the meanwhile, move on to making the cobbler.
- Preheat oven to 375 F (191 Celsius). Stir the flours, salt, and sugar in a large mixing bowl. Grate cold butter into the flour mixture with medium holes in the box grater so the butter is fine enough but still somewhat chunky and cold. Add milk and vanilla, and knead with your hands. Do not over mix, though. Throw in the blueberries and knead carefully a bit more until crumbly. Spread on a baking pan and bake for approximately 14-16 minutes. Let it cool.
- When three hours of freezing the ice cream are done, break up the cobber into small chunks and add them to the cream, stir it up a bit and mix briefly. Place loaf pan back in the freezer and freeze for another 3-4 hours. Serve and enjoy!

17. Blueberry Frozen Yoghurt

Serving: Serves 4 | Prep: | Cook: |Ready in:

Ingredients

- 1 cup full fat Greek style yoghurt
- 1/3 cup whipping cream (or half and half cream and crème fraiche)
- 5 teaspoons corn syrup
- 5 tablespoons frozen blueberries

Direction

- Whiz all the ingredients very briefly in a small blender or a food processor. If you have an ice cream machine, transfer the lot into it and churn as per the appliance instructions.
- If you don't have the ice cream maker, leave the mix in the blender and place the blender in the freezer.
- Take it out three to four times at an hour's intervals and whiz briefly again; taste for sweetness and add more corn syrup if necessary.
- After the last spin scrape the mix into a plastic container and keep in the freezer.
- The fro-yo needs to be taken out of the freezer to room temperature about 10 minutes before serving or moved to the fridge 20 minutes before.

18. Brandywine Tomato And Watermelon Granita With Agave Mint Syrup

Serving: Serves approx. 2 cups | Prep: | Cook: |Ready in:

Ingredients

- Brandywine Tomato and Watermelon Granita
- 3 cups 1-inch watermelon cubes, seeds removed
- 1 cup peeled, seeded, and chopped brandywine tomato
- 1/3 cup sugar
- 1 tablespoon minced crystalized ginger
- juice of one lemon
- 1 teaspoon lemon zest
- Agave-Mint Syrup
- 1/2 cup light agave nectar
- 8-12 fresh mint leaves

Direction

- For the Granita: In a food processor, process watermelon and next five ingredients together until smooth. Strain, pressing to extract liquid.
- Pour into a non-metallic shallow wide pan and freeze for one hour. Stir with a fork and freeze

for another hour. Stir and freeze for one more hour or until firm.

- Stir once more and serve in cups drizzled with Agave-Mint Syrup and garnished with fresh mint sprig and lemon, if desired.
- Warm agave nectar and mint leaves together gently over low heat. Remove from heat and let steep for five minutes. Carefully remove mint, scraping syrup off mint leaves if necessary. Serve with Brandywine Tomato and Watermelon Granita.

19. Brie Fig Ice Cream

Serving: Makes "generous 1 quart" | Prep: | Cook: | Ready in:

Ingredients

- Brie Ice Cream Mix
- 2 cups whole milk
- 1 tablespoon 1 tsn cornstarch
- 6 ounces brie cheese, rind removed
- 2 tablespoons Naefchatel cheese
- 1.25 cups heavy cream
- 2/3 cup sugar
- 1/4 cup light corn syrup
- 1 fig sauce
- Fig Sauce
- 3/4 cup fresh fig seeds (druplets)
- 2 tablespoons sugar

Direction

- Mix about 2 tbsp milk with cornstarch in small bowl to make a smooth slurry," divide brie and Naefchatel cheese into tiny pieces and mix together in a large bowl
- Combine remaining milk, the cream, sugar, and corn syrup in a 4 quart saucepan, bring to a rolling boil over m-h heat and boil for 4 min. Remove from heat & gradually whisk in cornstarch slurry, bring mixture back to boiling over m-h heat, stirring with a rubber

spatula until thickened, about 1 min. remove from heat"

- Gradually whisk hot milk mixture into cheese mixture until smooth." whisk well with each small addition of the hot milk mixture to ensure smoothness. Cover and chill in refrigerator while ice cream make in freezer overnight.
- Pour ice cream based into frozen ice cream maker until thick and creamy. Pack... into storage container, alternating with" fig sauce. "Do not mix. Press a sheet of" wax paper "directly against the surface, and seal with an airtight lid." Freeze overnight
- Fig Sauce
- Heat in small saucepan over medium high heat until well combined, remove from heat and allow it to cool before use. If making for brie ice cream, it's best to make before ice cream is put into ice cream maker. It can cool as you are spinning the ice cream.

20. Brown Butter Maple Pecan Ice Cream (Made With Dry Ice)

Serving: Makes 1 quart | Prep: | Cook: | Ready in:

Ingredients

- 8 ounces raw pecans (about 2 cups chopped)
- 12 tablespoons butter (1.5 sticks)
- 0.75 cups grade B maple syrup
- 2.5 cups milk
- 0.5 teaspoons salt
- 1 pound dry ice

Direction

- Brown the butter. In a medium saucepan, melt the butter over medium heat. The butter will foam as the water content evaporates; continue to cook the butter, swirling the pan every 15 to 30 seconds, until the foaming subsides and the butter starts to smell nutty. The moment that brown particles start to appear at the bottom of the saucepan, pull it off the heat but continue to swirl the pan for about 15 seconds.

- Off the heat, drop the pecans into the butter. This will cool the temperature of the butter (preventing it from burning and making it easier to handle) and add a roasted note to the pecans by frying them. Let the mixture sit for about 3-4 minutes.
- Add all the pecans and butter to a food processor, making sure you scrape all the brown bits at the bottom of the pan into the food processor as well. Process until very smooth, about 5 minutes.
- While you wait for the pecan butter to come together, prepare the dry ice. Wrap in a towel, and use a rolling pin or some other club-like implement (I used a baseball bat) to pulverize the dry ice into a powder. It's okay if some chunks remain.
- With the food processor running, drop in the salt through the spout. Slowly drizzle the maple syrup through the spout. Follow that with the milk.
- With the food processor running, add the dry ice one spoonful at a time through the spout. The dry ice will produce vapors out of the spout. DO NOT COVER THE SPOUT BETWEEN ADDITIONS. If you add too much as once, the mixture will bubble out of the spout; wait for most of the vapor coming out of the spout to dissipate before adding another spoonful.
- When the food processor begins to struggle, turn it off and quickly scoop out the ice cream into a freezable container, preferably one that has already been thoroughly chilled. Place the container in the freezer.
- Every couple of hours, you will need to stir the ice cream to help the excess carbon dioxide sublimate out. Otherwise, your ice cream will taste carbonated. Alternatively, you can let it sit in the freezer and let it release the excess gas on its own, but from past experience this can take up to a week.

21. Buttermilk Ice Cream With Plum Juniper Berry Swirl

Serving: Makes a quart of ice cream | Prep: | Cook: | Ready in:

Ingredients

- Plum Juniper Berry Syrup
- 2 1/2 cups plums, cleaned, pitted and quartered with skins left on, I used 5 Methley plums
- 1/2 cup sugar
- 4 whole juniper berries
- 1/2 cup water
- The Custard
- 1/1/2 cups heavy cream
- 1/2 cup whole milk
- 1 cup full fat buttermilk
- 1/2 cup sugar
- 5 egg yolks
- 1 tablespoon clear corn syrup

Direction

- Plum Juniper Berry Syrup
- Place everything in saucepan, bring to a boil then reduce heat to med and let cook until thick and plums are broken down and it's reduced by approximately 1/4 it takes about 15-20 minutes. Strain into a jar with a lid, pressing the plums leaving only the pulp and skin, let come to room temperature then refrigerate until ready to use. It's pretty thick and when it's cooled it's like the consistency of loose jam.
- Before you pour custard into the ice cream maker add the tbsp. of corn syrup to the custard, pour into ice cream maker following manufacturer's instruction. When it's ready it will be the consistency of soft serve ice cream. Put half of the custard into a freezer container, drizzle some of the syrup over the ice cream (I used 1/4 cup) and using a bamboo skewer or butter knife, swirl into the ice cream. Put the other half of the ice cream on top of it and

swirl more syrup. Freeze until it is a scoopable consistency.

- The Custard
- In heavy non-reactive saucepan heat cream, milk and buttermilk to scalding. Beat egg yolks and sugar with a whisk or electric mixer until light in color and thick. Slowly add some of the hot milk to the egg yolk mixture whisking constantly. Whisk to combine and add to the pan with the hot milk whisking constantly. Heat over med/hi heat until it becomes thick (165-170 degrees) and coats the back of the spoon, to test it swipe finger making a line, if it's done the line will remain intact. NOTE: if you don't have or cannot find full fat buttermilk use the low fat, omit the whole milk and increase heavy cream to 2 cups.
- Pour into heat proof container, cover with plastic directly onto the custard. Let cool at room temperature then refrigerate overnight or until it reaches 40 degrees. You can also prepare an ice bath, pour the custard into a zip lock bag, seal it well and immerse in the ice cold bath until it's cooled. Then refrigerate or use right away

22. CAPPUCCINO ICE CREAM

Serving: Makes 1 quart | Prep: | Cook: | Ready in:

Ingredients

- 3 cups heavy cream
- 12 tablespoons sugar, divided
- 3 large egg yolks
- 2 tablespoons powdered instant espresso
- 1/4 teaspoon vanilla extract
- 1 teaspoon unsweetened cocoa powder
- 1/2 teaspoon cinnamon
- 1 small block of high quality dark chocolate, shaved
- Kahlua, to taste

Direction

- MAKE SWEET WHIPPED CREAM: In a large bowl, beat cream until smooth. Gradually add 6 tablespoons of the sugar, beating until soft peaks form.
- IN ANOTHER BOWL, MIX THE REST: In a separate bowl, beat egg yolks with remaining 6 tablespoons of sugar until light in color. Add espresso, vanilla, cocoa powder, and cinnamon. Beat until combined.
- COMBINE AND FREEZE: Fold whipped cream into the egg mixture. Spoon mixture into an ice cream maker. Freeze according to the manufacturers' directions and then place in freezer until frozen.
- SERVE: Serve scoops of ice cream with dark chocolate shavings on top. Pour a bit of Kahlua over the top for the adults.

23. Caramel Fudge Brownie Chocolate Ice Cream

Serving: Serves 4 | Prep: | Cook: | Ready in:

Ingredients

- 200 milliliters whole milk
- 380 milliliters heavy cream
- 325 grams sugar
- 1 pinch salt
- 3 teaspoons cornstarch
- 50 grams cream cheese
- 40 grams cocoa powder
- 60 grams dark chocolate
- 2 tablespoons unsalted butter
- 1 egg
- 45 grams sifted all-purpose flour

Direction

- For the caramel ripple sprinkle 100gr sugar evenly over the bottom of a heavy-duty 4-quart saucepan, set it over low heat and cook barely stirring only when the inner layer of sugar starts to melt, mix the liquefied sugar with the crystallized sugar on top of it very gently. When all of the sugar is liquefied, continue cooking on low stirring until the caramel is penny-bronze in color. Take off heat, slowly add 180ml heavy cream a little at a time, stirring constantly until fully incorporated. If there are any lumps of hardened caramel left, return to low heat and cook stirring until completely melted. Take off heat, add a pinch of salt, cool to room temperature and store in a sealed jug until ready to use.

- For the small batch fudge brownies melt together 30gr dark chocolate, unsalted butter in a glass or metal bowl in a Bain Marie set over a pot of simmering water. When the chocolate and the butter have melted completely, take the bowl off the Bain Marie, stir in 100gr sugar, 1/6tsp salt, 1 large egg, 20gr sifted cocoa powder and the sifted flour, stir until smooth. Transfer to a 10x10cm buttered and parchment-lined pan. Bake at 175°C for 20 minutes.
- For the chocolate sauce in a small saucepan over medium heat combine 80ml water, 45gr sugar, 20gr sifted cocoa powder, cook 2min stirring until uniform. Add 30gr chopped dark chocolate, cook until completely melted and glossy.
- Dissolve the cornstarch in 50ml whole milk, leave to rest.
- In another small saucepan over medium heat combine 200ml heavy cream, the leftover milk, 80gr sugar, pinch salt, stir, bring to an almost boil, add the cornstarch milk and cook constantly stirring until thickened. Take off heat, add the cream cheese and the chocolate sauce, stir until smooth and combined. Cool to room temperature, then transfer into the fridge overnight.
- Freeze the ice cream according to the manufacturer's instructions adding small, uniformly cut cubes of brownies (a little less than a half of the amount you prepared) at the last couple of minutes of churning. Store in an airtight container swirling in pockets of the caramel sauce (a little less than a half the

amount you prepared) and store in the freezer for at least 4hours until firm enough to scoop.

24. Caramelized Balsamic Gelato

Serving: Makes about a quart | Prep: | Cook: |Ready in:

Ingredients

- Cream Custard Base
- 6 Large Egg Yolks
- 1.75 cups Whole Milk
- 1 cup Heavy Cream
- Balsamic Caramel Sugar
- 1.5 cups Superfine Sugar
- 4.5 tablespoons Aged Balsamic Vinegar

Direction

- Cream Custard Base
- In a medium sauce pot over medium heat, heat cream and whole milk to a slight scald. Set aside.
- Crack and separate egg yolks into a large metal bowl. Beat slightly to break up and set aside.
- Temper a small amount of hot cream into eggs to even the temperature and prevent burning. Add remaining cream very slowly in 3 or 4 portions, stirring the entire time for even blending.
- Place your bowl over a large sauce pot of just simmering water to cook. Cook 8 to 12 minutes until the custard begins to thicken, scraping and skimming the bottom and sides with a rubber spatula to prevent burning and "scrambled eggs." The desired consistency will cling lightly to the spatula and hold a line drawn through it with your finger (on the spatula.) Remove from heat.
- Strain the cooked custard to remove any lumps. Cover with plastic wrap in contact with the surface and set aside.
- Balsamic Caramel Sugar

- In a small to medium sauce pot over medium high heat, heat sugar to melting, washing down the sides with water with a pastry brush as needed to prevent crystals forming.
- Cook until the sugar begins to turn a medium golden brown. Working as quickly as you can, swirl once and add your vinegar all at once. Swirl again to mix and douse the bottom of the pot in icy water to stop cooking.
- Slowly pour the caramel into the cream base, stirring to prevent overheating. Continue stirring until all of the caramel has dissolved and you have a nice even light coffee color.
- Strain your completed custard one final time and place in the fridge near the back overnight for cold hydration.
- Pour chilled custard into your ice cream or gelato machine and churn on low speed for 10 to 15 minutes until it looks like soft serve. Pour into a freezer safe container and chill to set 4-6 hours.
- Enjoy!

25. Caramelized Pineapple Ice Cream

Serving: Makes 1.5 l | Prep: | Cook: |Ready in:

Ingredients

- Ice Cream
- 2 eggs
- 3/4 cup white sugar
- 3 cups half-and-half cream
- 1/2 teaspoon pure vanilla extract
- Toasted coconut (optional garnish)
- Caramelized Pineapple
- 3 cups fresh pineapple tidbits
- 2 tablespoons butter
- 3 tablespoons brown sugar
- 2 tablespoons rum

Direction

- Ice Cream

- In a heavy saucepan, lightly whisk together the eggs and sugar.
- Add 2 cups of the half-and-half cream.
- Cook the mixture over medium-low heat stirring constantly, until the mixture is thick enough to coat the back of a wooden spoon (170 degrees F / 77 degrees C).
- Remove from heat immediately and add the remaining half-and-half to stop the cooking. Let cool slightly. Stir in the vanilla.
- Cool and chill overnight in the fridge.
- Caramelized Pineapple
- While the ice cream is chilling, prepare the caramelized pineapple. Melt the butter in a non-stick pan.
- Add the pineapple tidbits and the brown sugar.
- Cook over medium heat, stirring occasionally, until the pineapple turns a beautiful, caramel color and all the juice has turned thick and saucy. This should take about 13 minutes.
- Stir in the rum.
- Cool and chill overnight in the fridge.
- To finish, pour the custard into an ice cream maker and prepare according to the manufacturer's instructions.
- In the final moments of churning, add the caramelized pineapple and churn to distribute throughout the ice cream.
- Garnish with toasted coconut if desired.

26. Celery Prosecco Pops, Citrus Gelatine

Serving: Serves 8-10 | Prep: | Cook: |Ready in:

Ingredients

- Celery and Prosecco Pops
- 8 ounces sugar
- 8 ounces water
- 10 3 inch parsley stems (optional for garnish)
- 6 bright green celery stalks
- 1 cup Prosecco

- 2 tablespoons freshly squeezed lemon juice or to taste
- Citrus Gelatine
- 1 1/2 cups various citrus fruit segments (see intro)
- 1 cup freshly squeezed orange juice
- 1/4 cup sugar
- 3 sheets of gelatin

Direction

- Celery and Prosecco Pops
- If making the parsley garnish preheat the oven to 60 degrees C 120 (F). Make a simple syrup with the sugar and water. When the syrup is ready add the parsley stems and bring to a boil. Simmer for 3 minutes. Cover the pan with a plate and let the stems cool in the syrup for one hour. Remove the stems to a parchment lined baking sheet and bake for two hours or until the stems are dry.
- Meanwhile, remove the first inch or two from the base of each celery stalk (where the color is paler) and reserve for another use. Cut the remaining celery into 1/2 inch pieces and add to the syrup along with the prosecco. Bring the syrup back to the boil then simmer gently for 8-10 minutes.
- Transfer to a blender and add celery or lovage leaves. Whiz. Push through a fine sieve and discard the solids. Add lemon juice to taste to the syrup and pour into popsicle molds, ice cube trays or silpat molds of your choice. Freeze.
- Citrus Gelatin
- Layer the citrus segments into a cling film lined loaf tin or silpat mold. Soften the gelatin in cold water.
- Bring the sugar and juice to the boil and remove from the heat. Stir in the softened gelatin. Pour over fruit and refrigerate until set.
- To Serve: Slice the gelatin with a sharp knife and top with a celery pop. Garnish with the candied parsley stem if using.

27. Ch Ch Ch Cherry Bomb Gelato

Serving: Serves 4-6 | Prep: 9hours0mins | Cook: 1hours0mins | Ready in:

Ingredients

- 4 cups whole milk (divided, 3 plus 1)
- enough pitted cherries to yield 1 1/4 cup puree. You will need about 2 1/4/ cups to begin with. Use more if necessary.
- 3 tablespoons corn starch
- 2 tablespoons corn syrup
- 1/4 cup dry milk powder
- 1/8 teaspoon kosher salt (do not use sea salt)
- 2 tablespoons honey
- 1/2 cup heavy cream
- Amarena cherries in syrup*; allow one serving spoon per portion of gelato.

Direction

- Using a small food processor chop the pitted cherries until you have a coarse puree. Set aside.
- Fill a large bowl with ice (big enough to hold the second bowl)
- Using the smaller bowl, whisk one cup milk with the corn starch to dissolve.
- Combine the sugar, milk powder, corn syrup and salt with the remaining three cups milk in a deep sauce pan and heat to the scalding point. Do not boil.
- Add the contents of the other bowl to this. Bring back to heat until viscous.
- Add this back to the smaller bowl and whisk in the cherry puree. Allow to cool down nested in the ice bowl. Cover and seal and hold in the refrigerator for at least four hours, or better still overnight.
- Depending on your ice cream maker you may have to freeze the machine bowl overnight. Don't forget to do this.
- On the day you are ready to make your gelato add the heavy cream and honey to the milk/fruit blend. Whisk together and pour

into the frozen bowl of the machine which you have already fitted with the dasher. Run the machine until you have a nice texture, perhaps as long as 20 or 25 minutes depending on the machine.

- Scoop into serving bowls and top each portion with the amarena cherries. This will heighten the sweetness.
- Amarena cherries can be found in Italian specialty shops and many supermarkets. They are a product of the Bologna area. Italian maraschinos are a good substitute, e.g. Luxardo. American maraschino are a poor imitation of the real thing.

28. Cherry Espresso Balsamic Brownie Bites

Serving: Makes 1 small batch, about 12 brownies | Prep: | Cook: | Ready in:

Ingredients

- 1 1/4 cups raw pecans
- 3 ounces exquisite quality dark chocolate, 55-70%
- 1 ounce shot of strong espresso
- 1 tablespoon balsamic vinegar
- 1/4 teaspoon vanilla salt
- 3/4 cup dried cherries, divided

Direction

- Combine all ingredients, reserving half the cherries, in a food processor.
- Blend until mostly smooth.
- Stir in remaining cherries.
- Press into a parchment lined baking dish and chill until set.
- Easily remove brownies and parchment from the baking dish and cut into desired sized "bites."

29. Chinatown Ice Cream

Serving: Makes about 1 quart | Prep: | Cook: | Ready in:

Ingredients

- 2 cups milk
- 1 cup heavy cream
- 1 cinnamon stick
- 3 cloves
- 5 whole black peppercorns
- 1/2 teaspoon fennel seeds
- 1 14 oz can red kidney beans, drained and rinsed
- 1/2 cup dark brown sugar, packed
- 1/2 teaspoon vanilla extract
- 1 teaspoon almond extract
- pinch of salt

Direction

- Combine milk, cream, granulated sugar, spices and a pinch of salt in a medium saucepan. Puree the kidney beans with the dark brown sugar in a food processor (you can add a tablespoon or two of the milk/cream mixture to get it going) and add to the milk mixture. Cook over medium heat, stirring frequently, until steaming and almost to a simmer, but do not allow to boil. Cook 5-7 minutes, until the mixture coats the back of a wooden spoon, stirring constantly.
- Remove from the heat and add the vanilla and almond extracts. Cover the pan and allow the spices to steep, until cooled to room temperature.
- Remove the cloves, peppercorns, and cinnamon stick from the milk mixture (I do not strain as I like the bean texture and the whole fennel seeds in my final product.) Add to an ice cream maker and churn according to the manufacturer's instructions (generally about 20 minutes). You can eat it like soft serve at this point, or place in a lidded container place in the freezer for one hour to firm up.

30. Chocolate Chip Cookie Ice Cream Sandwiches

Serving: Makes 12 sandwiches | Prep: 0hours20mins | Cook: 0hours20mins | Ready in:

Ingredients

- 1 cup unsalted butter, softened to room temperature
- 3/4 cup granulated sugar
- 3/4 cup light brown sugar
- 2 large eggs
- 2 teaspoons pure vanilla extract
- 1 1/4 cups all-purpose flour
- 1 1/4 cups bread flour
- 1 teaspoon baking soda
- 1/2 teaspoon salt
- 1 quart your favorite ice cream

Direction

- Preheat oven to 350°F. Line large baking sheets with parchment paper or silicone baking mats. Set aside.
- In a large bowl using a hand-held mixer or stand mixer with the paddle attachment, beat the butter on medium speed until completely smooth and creamy. Add the sugar and light brown sugar and mix on medium speed until fluffy and light in color. Mix in eggs one at a time and scrape down the sides and bottom of the bowl after each addition. Mix in vanilla.
- In a separate bowl, sift together flours, baking soda and salt. On low speed, slowly add flour mixture into butter mixture until combined.
- Add the chocolate chips and mix by hand just until evenly distributed.
- Scoop dough, about 3 tablespoons each, and place on prepared baking sheets leaving 2 inches between each cookie. Bake 16-18 minutes, until edges are golden brown. Remove from oven and allow to cool for 2 minutes on the cookie sheet. Transfer to a cooling rack and cool completely.
- Place a scoop of ice cream on a cookie and top with a second cookie. Gently push down and repeat with the rest of the cookies. Freeze sandwiches at least 1 hour before serving.

31. Chocolate Raspberry Baked Alaska

Serving: Serves 12-16 | Prep: | Cook: | Ready in:

Ingredients

- Brownie Layer
- Scant ½ cup vegetable oil (3.25 oz)
- 1 cup sugar
- 2 tablespoons dark brown sugar
- 3/4 cup good quality unsweetened cocoa powder
- 1/2 teaspoon salt
- 1/4 cup amaretto
- 2 teaspoons vanilla extract
- 2 large eggs
- 1/2 cup almond flour/almond meal
- 1/3 cup chocolate chips, melted
- Raspberry Layer and Meringue
- For the Raspberry Parfait
- 2 12-oz bags frozen raspberries, thawed with juices
- 8 large egg yolks
- 3/4 cup sugar
- 2/3 cup amaretto
- For the Meringue
- 8 large egg whites (these will not be fully cooked in this recipe so if that is of concern use pasteurized egg whites)
- 2 cups sugar

Direction

- Brownie Layer
- Preheat the oven to 325. Line a 9×9 square pan with parchment or foil, leaving an overhang on two sides. Spray the pan liberally with cooking spray. Set aside
- Combine the oil, sugars, cocoa, amaretto, salt and vanilla in the bowl of an electric mixer. Add the eggs one at a time, beating well after

each addition. Add the almond flour and beat at high speed for 2 minutes. Stir in the melted chocolate.

- Pour into the prepared pan. Bake for approximately 25 minutes or until a tester near the middle of the pan comes out with lots of moist crumbs. They will seem underdone, that is correct. Let the brownies cool completely in the pan.
- Remove the brownies from pan by lifting them out with the parchment/foil overhang. Cut the brownie in half into two 9 x 4.5 inch pieces. Set aside. (Can be made up to two days in advance, further if the brownies are frozen)
- Raspberry Layer and Meringue
- To make the raspberry layer:
- Line 2 9 x 4.5 inch loaf pans with plastic wrap or parchment paper and set aside. (If using ice cream instead of the raspberry parfait skip to step 10)
- Puree the berries in food processor. Strain through a sieve set over large measuring cup, pressing in solids in strainer to extract as much puree as possible. Alternatively, pass the raspberries through a food mill to remove the seeds. Cover puree and chill until cold, at least 1 hour and up to 1 day.
- Combine egg yolks, amaretto and sugar in a medium metal bowl. Set over saucepan of simmering water (do not allow the bottom of the bowl to touch the water). Whisk constantly until thick and billowy and candy thermometer registers 160, about 7 minutes. (If you do not have a candy thermometer it should feel hot to the touch)
- Remove bowl from water. Add 1 ¾ cup cold berry puree. Using an electric mixer beat mixture until cool, about 7 minutes.
- Pour raspberry mixture into prepared baking pans. (It using ice cream soften it slightly and then spread it into an even layer in the pans) Top each pan with one piece of the brownie. Cover, freeze until firm, at least 6 hours.
- To Make the Meringue
- Place the egg whites and sugar in the metal bowl of an electric mixer. Place the bowl over a pan of simmering water and stir constantly

until the sugar is dissolved and the mixture is warm to the touch, 2-3 minutes. Transfer bowl to the mixer and whip (using the whisk attachment) until the mixture holds a stiff peak. (Depending on the size of the mixing bowl this may need to be done in two batches)

- Remove one of the loaf pans from the freezer. Invert it onto a cookie sheet and remove the plastic wrap. Working quickly, spread ½ the meringue on the frozen loaf, making sure to cover it completely and seal the edges. Return it to the freezer and repeat with the second loaf. (The baked Alaskas can be made up to this point a day ahead. Keep frozen until ready to serve.)
- Right before serving remove the baked Alaskas from the freezer. Place them under the broiler for 1-2 minutes or until the outsides are lightly toasted. This can also be done using a kitchen torch. Serve immediately.
- Note: In order to make individual baked Alaskas double the brownie and meringue recipes. Use 2.5-3 inch dessert rings to cut out circles in the brownie. Leave the brownie in the dessert ring and fill to the top with the raspberry filling. Once frozen remove the rings and carefully coat each dessert with the meringue. Makes approximately 12 (depending on the size of the dessert rings).

32. Chocolate And Olive Oil Ice Cream Sandwiches

Serving: Makes about 10 sandwiches | Prep: | Cook: | Ready in:

Ingredients

- Olive Oil Gelato with Cacao Nibs
- 3/4 cup sugar
- 6 tablespoons water
- 3/4 cup milk
- pinch salt
- 4 egg yolks

- 6 tablespoons olive oil
- 2 tablespoons cacao nibs
- Salted Chocolate Rye Cookies
- 1/2 pound chopped bittersweet chocolate
- 2 tablespoons unsalted butter
- 6 tablespoons dark rye flour
- 1/2 teaspoon baking soda
- 1/4 teaspoon salt
- 3/4 cup muscovado or dark brown sugar
- 2 eggs
- 1 1/2 teaspoons vanilla extract
- flaky salt, such as Maldon, for sprinkling

Direction

- Olive Oil Gelato with Cacao Nibs
- Whisk the sugar, water, milk and salt together in a medium saucepan. Bring the mixture to a simmer, stirring occasionally to dissolve the sugar. While the mixture is heating on the stove, whisk the egg yolks together in a large bowl.
- When the milk mixture has come to a gentle simmer, slowly stream it into the egg yolks while whisking constantly. Pour the mixture back into the saucepan and cook over medium low heat while whisking constantly until the mixture comes to 185°F. Be careful not to let the mixture boil which will scramble the eggs and ruin the base.
- Remove the custard from the heat and chill completely. When you are ready to churn the ice cream, whisk in the olive oil. The mixture will be thick and glossy. Churn the custard in an ice cream machine according to manufacturer's instructions, adding the cacao nibs just before the ice cream is done spinning. Remove to a freezer safe container and freeze until firm, 4 hours or overnight.
- Salted Chocolate Rye Cookies
- Melt the chocolate and butter together over a double boiler. Stir occasionally until the mixture is completely smooth. Remove from the heat and set aside while you prepare the rest of the cookies
- In the bowl of a standing mixer fitted with the whisk attachment or with an electric mixer, beat the eggs. Slowly add in the sugar and beat until the mixture is light in color and the eggs have tripled in volume.
- Stir in the vanilla extract, followed by the melted chocolate mixture. Finally, remove the bowl from the mixer and fold in the flour mixture until well combined. The dough will be very soft, almost batter-like in texture. Refrigerate the dough for about 30 minutes or until firm enough to scoop.
- Preheat oven to 350°. Line a baking sheet with parchment paper and portion the cookies into heaping tablespoons. Sprinkle each cookie with flaky salt and bake the cookies for 8-10 minutes or until the cookies have puffed and crackly tops. Let the cookies cool on the baking sheets for 5 minutes then move to a rack to cool completely.
- When the cookies have cooled completely and the ice cream is firm enough to scoop, assemble the sandwiches.
- To Assemble: Flip half of the cookies over so their flat sides are up. Top each cookie with a small scoop of ice cream (a cookie scoop makes a great mini ice cream scoop) and top the ice cream with another cookie, flat side down. Put the sandwiches on a parchment lined baking sheet or plate and re-freeze until firm.

---

33. Chocolate Cookie Chunk Cheesecake Ice Cream With And A Gooey Cinnamon Ripple

Serving: Serves 4 | Prep: | Cook: | Ready in:

Ingredients

- 300 grams cream cheese
- 180 grams 20%-fat sour cream
- 125 milliliters pouring cream
- 130 grams sugar
- 200 grams light brown sugar
- 1 pinch salt

- 3 tablespoons all-purpose flour
- 1,25 teaspoons ground cinnamon
- 1/2 teaspoon vanilla bean powder
- 1 tablespoon unsalted butter
- 70 grams chocolate shortbread cookie crumbs

Direction

- For the cinnamon sauce in a small saucepan over medium heat combine the brown sugar, the flour and 180ml hot water, cook until uniform, add the butter and 3/4tsp cinnamon powder, cook until thickened and smooth. Cool and store in an airtight container until ready to use.
- For the ice cream in a blender combine the cream cheese, sour cream, thin pouring cream, sugar, 1/2 cinnamon powder and the vanilla bean powder, whizz away until really smooth and creamy. Chill in the fridge overnight.
- Freeze in your ice cream maker according to the manufacturer's instructions adding the crushed chocolate cookies at the last couple of minutes of churning. Spoon into an airtight container alternating layers of ice cream and the cinnamon sauce (6-8tsp), store in the fridge for at least 5 hours until set.

34. Cinnamon And Ancho Chile Scented Avocado Ice Cream

Serving: Serves 8 | Prep: | Cook: | Ready in:

Ingredients

- 2 cups heavy cream
- 1 cup milk
- 6 egg yolks
- 3/4 cup granulated sugar
- 1 pinch sea salt
- 1 teaspoon vanilla extract
- 3 ripe Hass avocados
- 2 ounces freshly squeezed lemon juice
- 1/2 teaspoon ground ancho chile powder
- 1/2 teaspoon ground cinnamon

Direction

- Over medium heat, scald the cream and milk. Be careful not to let it boil over.
- Meanwhile, in large bowl, whisk together the yolks, sugar, salt and vanilla until light and creamy. Add a small amount of hot cream to yolks, whisking quickly to temper the egg mixture. Gradually whisk in remaining cream. Place mixture over a water bath, whisking constantly, until mixture has thickened enough to coat the back of a spoon.
- Remove from the water bath, placing the bowl immediately into an ice bath. Stirring occasionally, cool the mixture, then strain into another bowl. Cover and chill for at least one hour. This can be made up to two days ahead.
- While custard is cooling, scoop the flesh of the avocados into food processor or blender. Add the lemon juice, ancho chile powder and cinnamon. Process until very smooth, stopping to scrape down sides as needed. Place the avocado mixture in refrigerator to chill along with the custard.
- When ready to make the ice cream, stir the avocado and custard together, until well blended. Following the instructions for your ice cream maker, freeze the ice cream.

35. Coconut Ice Cream With Forbidden Rice And Saigon Cinnamon

Serving: Serves 4 | Prep: | Cook: | Ready in:

Ingredients

- 1/2 cup glutinous black rice
- 1/4 cup sugar
- 2 cans coconut milk
- 2-3 sticks saigon cinnamon
- 1/4 cup sugar

Direction

- Soak glutinous black rice overnight. Drain next day and rinse.
- Put rice in a small pot. Add 1 cup of water to grains, bring to boil and then let simmer for about 15-20 mins. Check to see if rice is chewy/done, drain extra water if it is and put back on heat.
- Add 1/4 cup sugar and stir on low heat. Heat for about 3-5mins with lid off or until water has evaporated and rice is sticky. Allow to cool.
- Shake up 2 cans of coconut milk so the fat layer is mixed well. Put in medium pot with 1/4 cup sugar and heat to simmer (but not boiling).
- Take off heat and stir in vanilla and cinnamon sticks. Allow to cool. Strain or fish out cinnamon sticks. Chill in fridge overnight or at least 3 hours and cover with plastic wrap on surface.
- Freeze coconut mixture in an ice cream machine according to the manufacturer's instructions. When done churning (nice and soft), add as much of the prepared sticky black rice as you like.
- Stick it in the fridge to firm up.

36. Coconut Kaffir Lime Ice Cream

Serving: Serves 2 | Prep: | Cook: |Ready in:

Ingredients

- Kaffir lime syrup
- 350 grams brown rice syrup
- 10   fresh kaffir lime leaves
- Kaffir lime coconut ice cream
- 400 grams coconut milk
- 50 grams coconut oil
- 100 grams infused rice syrup
- Pinch salt
- 1   pineapple

Direction

- To make the infused sugar syrup gently heat brown rice syrup in a pan, keep on a low heat for 20 minutes, turn off and let sit for 2 hours to infuse.
- Blend ingredients together for the ice cream (excluding the pineapple), chill and churn according to manufacturer guidelines.
- If you don't have an ice cream machine, place in the freezer in a covered container, take out and blend 3-4 times throughout the first few hours of freezing.
- Roast pineapple:
- Pre heat over 220c. Peel and core your pineapple, cut into eighths and quarter each slice. Place in a lined roasting tray. Drizzle over 4 tablespoons of the syrup.
- Roast for 30 minutes until soft and beginning to caramelize.
- To serve. Scoop the coconut ice cream into bowls, top with roast pineapple and a spoonful of the syrup and enjoy.

37. Coconut Lime Sorbet

Serving: Serves 4 | Prep: | Cook: |Ready in:

Ingredients

- 1 15 oz. can coconut milk (organic is good)
- 2/3 cup grated jaggery
- 2-3   kaffir lime leaves
- 1/2 cup fresh lime juice
- 1 pinch sea salt

Direction

- In a medium saucepan over medium-low heat, combine coconut milk, jaggery and lime leaves. Stir until jaggery is dissolved and milk is heated through, about 5 minutes.
- Remove coconut milk from heat, cover pan and allow to steep as it cools. Once completely cool, stir in lime juice and strain, discarding lime leaves. Stir in salt.

- Process in your ice cream maker. Serve right away, or freeze for a couple of hours to firm up more, as desired.

38. Coffee Cardamom Ice Pops With Guittard Chocolate Powder

Serving: Makes about 8 ice pops | Prep: | Cook: |Ready in:

Ingredients

- 4-5 cups freshly brewed coffee (French press coffee works very well)
- 5-6 cardamom pods, seeds removed and lightly toasted
- 2 cups organic cream or soymilk
- 2-3 tablespoons honey
- 1/8 cup Guittard semi-sweet chocolate, finely crushed

Direction

- Toast the cardamom seeds in a dry sauté pan until fragrant. Add directly to the grounds and brew coffee.
- Combine the cardamom-infused coffee, cream and honey. Pour mixture into ice pop molds or 2 ounce glass cups and place in freezer for 1 1/2 hours.
- Remove from freezer. Once somewhat set, insert wooden ice pop sticks and dust the top of each ice pop with chocolate powder, pressing the chocolate gently to set.
- Place back in freezer for 3-4 + hours until completely frozen and set.
- Remove from molds and serve immediately.*
  Note: the coffee mixture can be made any way you enjoy by adding more/less cream and/or honey.

39. Concord Grape Sorbet

Serving: Makes about 4 cups | Prep: | Cook: |Ready in:

Ingredients

- 2.5 pounds concord grapes (measured after stems removed)
- 1/4 cup water
- 1/4 cup sugar
- 1/4 cup vodka
- 2 tablespoons fresh lemon juice (probably one large lemon)

Direction

- In a non-reactive pot (I used hard-anodized), simmer, covered, the cleaned grapes with water until the grapes get soft. By this point, the smell of grape juice will entice you back to the kitchen. Give the grapes a stir a few times to loosen the skins. This whole process took about 20 minutes.
- Pour the grape concoction into a fine-mesh sieve in batches, and push juice out into a bowl beneath, leaving any stems and seeds behind. I used a wooden spoon to press out as much juice as I could. I ended up with about 2.5 cups of pure grape juice.
- Add sugar, vodka, and lemon juice to the grape juice and whir a few times with an immersion blender to dissolve the sugar. You'll use the immersion blender again later.
- Pour the grape mix into a bowl, cake pan, or whatever you want and pop it into the freezer. The flatter the container, the quicker the sorbet will freeze. The more alcohol, the slower the sorbet will freeze. After about 2 hours, check on the sorbet. It should be about half frozen. Use the immersion blender to break up any icy bits. Return the sorbet to the freezer and repeat this every hour or so. If you forget and throw the sorbet in the freezer overnight, no problem – it will just take a few extra whirs with the blender to break up the solid mass the next morning.

40. Corn Ice Cream With Blueberry, Blackberry Compote

Serving: Serves 6 | Prep: | Cook: | Ready in:

Ingredients

- For the corn ice cream
- 2 cups heavy cream
- 1 1/2 cups whole milk
- 3 ears of sweet corn- about 3 cups, cobs reserved if using fresh
- 3/4 cup sugar
- 4 large egg yolks
- 1 teaspoon vanilla extract
- For the compote
- 1 cup blueberries (frozen is fine)
- 1 cup blackberries (frozen is fine)
- 2 tablespoons lemon juice
- 1 teaspoon lemon zest
- 1/2 cinnamon stick

Direction

- Remove the kernels of corn from the cob, keep the cobs.
- Bring the cream, corn, cobs, and milk to a simmer in a heavy bottomed pot over medium-low heat. Stir occasionally, and do not allow the mixture to boil- if it does boil you'll have to start again!
- Beat the ¾ cup sugar and egg yolks until the mixture becomes smooth and thick, and lightens in color. While the mixer is still on, slowly add 1 cup of the hot milk and cream mixture to the eggs to temper them.
- Transfer the egg mixture back into the pot, and continue to cook until thickened. The mixture will coat the back of a spoon (about 4-5 minutes). Remove from the heat, and stir in the vanilla extract.
- Transfer the mixture to a bowl in an ice water bath, and cover with plastic wrap. Be sure to press the plastic wrap down to the surface of the custard to prevent a skin on top.

Refrigerate overnight (but if you don't have patience like me-at least until the custard is chilled).

- Remove the cobs from the bowl and discard. Transfer the custard to a blender and blend until smooth (or until you puree the kernels to your desired consistency- I like to have the visual of corn kernels so I only pulse slightly). Transfer to an ice cream machine and follow the manufacturer's instructions. Freeze for at least 4 hours.
- For the compote: In a small saucepan add the berries, lemon juice and extract, cinnamon stick, and 2 tablespoons sugar on medium low heat. Smash with a fork or potato smasher until you get the thickness you desire. Cool and serve on top of the corn ice cream.

41. Crushed Meringue For Ice Cream Topping

Serving: Makes 2-3 cups | Prep: | Cook: | Ready in:

Ingredients

- 3 egg whites
- 1 cup sugar
- 2-3 tablespoons instant espresso or unsweetened cocoa, to taste
- Canola oil or another neutral-tasting oil for spraying
- Pinch of salt
- 1 teaspoon vanilla extract

Direction

- If using frozen egg whites, thaw them in the refrigerator.
- Mix the sugar with the instant espresso.
- Preheat the oven to 250 degrees F. Line a jelly roll pan with aluminum foil sprayed with oil.
- Beat the egg whites with a pinch of salt until they are very stiff, gradually adding the sugar and the vanilla.

- Spread the batter evenly onto the aluminum foil and bake for 60 minutes, until dry to the touch. Remove the pan from the oven and leave the oven on. Transfer the meringue onto a large cutting board and peel off the aluminum foil. It's OK if it breaks into many pieces, as it will be crushed anyway.
- Coarsely chop the meringue with a large knife and spread it out on the jelly roll pan. Bake for another 30 minutes, until the meringue has barely any moist spots left. Turn off the oven but leave the meringue in with the door closed, which will dry it further.
- After the meringue is cooled completely, store in tin cans. It keeps for several weeks.

42. Earl Grey Ice Cream With Blackberry Swirl

Serving: Makes 1 quart | Prep: | Cook: | Ready in:

Ingredients

- 1 1/2 ounces cream cheese
- 1/8 teaspoon fine sea salt
- 1 tablespoon 1 teaspoon cornstarch
- 2 cups 2% milk
- 1 1/4 cups heavy cream
- 1/2 cup sugar
- 1 1/2 tablespoons light corn syrup
- 2 tablespoons loose earl grey tea leaves (Rishi or same quality)
- 1 tablespoon plain vodka
- 1 tablespoon seedless blackberry jam

Direction

- Prep three bowls, a small, medium and a large one. Place cream cheese and salt into the medium bowl, mash with a fork, and set aside. In the small bowl, mix the cornstarch and 2 tbsp of the milk. Set this slightly thickened paste aside.
- In a large pot, add the rest of the milk and cream with the corn syrup and sugar. Bring to

a boil over a medium heat. On a simmer, continue stirring for about 4 minutes and no more. Remove the pot from heat, stir in the cornstarch mixture and bring this back to a boil for an additional minute, stirring constantly until the mixture thickens slightly. Add in your loose tea leaves to the hot mixture and let steep for 5 minutes. You might be tempted to place the leaves in a cheesecloth, but placing them in directly will infuse the ice cream really well (you'll be straining this later anyway).

- Add a small amount of the boiled milk to the cream cheese, whisking well to incorporate and break up any cream cheese lumps. Once the cream cheese has smoothed out, add the rest of the boiled milk.
- Cool the ice cream completely over an ice bath set in the large bowl. Refrigerate the covered cooled mixture for at least 4 hours or overnight. While you might be impatient to just put the ice cream into the machine right away, chilling it completely will keep the ice cream from crystallizing (that weird chalky texture) while it's churning in the machine.
- Using a fine mesh strainer, pour the liquid through the strainer, pressing on the tea leaves to get all the ice cream out. Any cream cheese or solids that haven't been blended well will remain out and help make your ice cream smooth and creamy. Stir in the vodka to the liquid ice cream before pouring into your ice cream maker. Follow your ice cream manufacturer's instructions for the length of time, but it usually will take 20-30 minutes for the ice cream to start coming together.
- Line a glass container (e.g.: Pyrex) that comes with its own lid using saran wrap (long enough to cover, too) and place a layer of ice cream, drizzle some of the blackberry jam in thin streaks. Put in more ice cream and continue layering in the blackberry swirls. Cover the ice cream with the hanging saran again before placing the top on. Once you're ready to serve the ice cream, let it soften at room temperature for about 2 minutes. You'll know "it's ready" when you can scoop easily.

Scoop the ice cream from the perpendicular direction of your blackberry streaks, to create a swirly effect in your scoop.

43. Ferrero Rocher Lazy Cake With Vanilla Caramel Ice Cream

Serving: Serves 4 people | Prep: 0hours10mins | Cook: 0hours0mins | Ready in:

Ingredients

- 12 digestive biscuits
- 6 teaspoons high quality cocoa powder
- 80 grams butter, at room temperature
- 4 tablespoons icing sugar
- 3/4 cup whipping cream
- 1 teaspoon vanilla extract
- 1/4 cup chopped hazelnuts
- 5 Ferrero Rocher chocolate balls
- 4 scoops vanilla caramel ice cream

Direction

- In a bowl, mix butter, cocoa powder, icing sugar, whipping cream and vanilla extract till smooth and well incorporated. (To facilitate the process you can heat in the microwave for 30 seconds or in the oven for a minute).
- Add 1 later of digestive biscuits (3-4 biscuits) in a lined 15-inch round tin. Break some of the biscuits to fill the gaps.
- Add 1/3 of the cocoa mixture and garnish with some chopped hazelnuts.
- Repeat 2 more times.
- Freeze for 1 hour.
- Flip onto a serving dish & layer with vanilla ice cream, Ferrero Rocher chocolate and chopped hazelnuts.

44. Foolproof Ice Cream

Serving: Serves about 1 1/4 quarts | Prep: | Cook: | Ready in:

Ingredients

- 4 egg yolks
- 1.5 cups heavy cream
- 1.5 cups whole milk
- 3/4 cup sugar
- 1 vanilla bean

Direction

- Heat milk and cream in a small saucepan with some sugar to 175 degrees. (Use a candy thermometer!)
- Meanwhile, beat the yolks with the remaining sugar at least 2 min. with an electric mixer or 4 min. with a whisk until pale yellow.
- Slowly pour a small amount of the heated milk-cream-sugar mixture into the egg yolks, whisking constantly as you pour.
- Whisk the thinned egg yolks back into the saucepan containing the remaining milk-cream-sugar.
- Scrape the insides of the vanilla bean into the saucepan.
- Heat to 180 degrees.
- Pour the cooked custard through a fine mesh strainer into a container.
- Chill custard to 40 degrees or lower. (I usually make the custard right before I go to sleep so it can chill in my refrigerator overnight.)
- Churn for 30 mins. If you have any add-ins, add to the ice cream for the last 30 seconds.
- Put in the freezer in an air-tight container for 2-4 hours to harden completely.
- 30 mins. before serving, transfer from the freezer to the fridge.

45. Fresh Mint And Spring Peas Ice Cream

Serving: Makes 1.25 l | Prep: | Cook: | Ready in:

Ingredients

- 3 cups peas (enough to yield 2 cups of puree)
- 1/2 cup tightly packed fresh mint leaves
- 1 tablespoon lemon juice
- 2 eggs
- 1/2 cup white sugar
- 1/4 cup honey
- 3 cups half-and-half cream, divided

Direction

- Bring a pot of water to boil (just enough water to cover the peas, once they are added to the pot). Add the peas, along with a pinch of sugar (no salt!), and boil until they are tender. This will take about 2 minutes for fresh peas and 3 minutes for frozen peas. Quickly drain the peas in a colander and transfer them to a bowl of ice water to stop the cooking and to preserve their bright green colour.
- Strain the peas and place them, the mint leaves, and 1/2 cup of the half and half cream into a blender and puree until smooth, scraping the sides down as required. If your blender is not super powerful, pass the puree through a fine sieve to remove any larger bits. You should have at least 2 cups of silky pea puree. Stir in the lemon juice.
- In a heavy saucepan, lightly whisk together the eggs and sugar.
- Add the honey and 2 cups of the half-and-half cream.
- Cook the mixture over medium-low heat stirring constantly, until the mixture is thick enough to coat the back of a wooden spoon (170 degrees F / 77 degrees C).
- Remove from heat immediately and add the remaining half-and-half to stop the cooking. Place the saucepan into an ice bath to cool the custard rapidly.
- When the custard is cool, whisk in the pea puree.
- Chill overnight in the fridge.
- Pour the custard into an ice cream maker and prepare according to the manufacturer's instructions.

46. Fresh Ricotta Ice Cream

Serving: Makes 1 scant quart | Prep: | Cook: | Ready in:

Ingredients

- 1 2/3 cups fresh, whole milk ricotta
- 3 ounces cream cheese
- 1 cup whole milk
- 1 cup sugar
- 2 tablespoons dark rum
- 1 teaspoon lemon zest, freshly grated
- 1/2 teaspoon vanilla
- 1/8 teaspoon salt
- 1 cup heavy cream
- 2-3 tablespoons chopped candied citrus peel (a combination of orange, lemon and citron)
- 2-3 tablespoons chopped pistachios
- 2-3 tablespoons chopped bittersweet chocolate

Direction

- Blend cheeses, milk, sugar, rum, zest, vanilla and salt in a blender until smooth. Add cream and blend until just combined.
- Freeze mixture in an ice cream maker, adding candied citrus peels, chocolate and pistachios at the end. Mix until just incorporated. Transfer to an airtight container and put in freezer to harden. Allow to sit a few minutes to soften before scooping!

47. Frozen Strawberry Cheesecake Pops

Serving: Makes 6 - 12 | Prep: | Cook: | Ready in:

Ingredients

- 300 grams strawberries
- 340 grams cream cheese
- 50 grams granulated sugar
- 115 grams whipping cream

Direction

- Slice each of 3 strawberries into 4 slices, and place a piece into 12 8cl paper cups (or 6 25cl cups).
- Place the remaining strawberries in a food processor, with the cream cheese, and sugar. Blend until smooth.
- In a medium bowl, beat the whipping cream with a hand mixer on high speed until soft peaks form. Gently stir the cream into the strawberry mixture.
- Spoon into the prepared cups, then gently tap them on the counter to remove any air bubbles. Insert a wooden pop stick into the center of each cup.
- Place in the freezer for 4 hours, or until firm. Remove the frozen pops from cups just before serving.

48. Frozen Strawberry Fluff Pie

Serving: Serves 16 | Prep: | Cook: | Ready in:

Ingredients

- For the filling:
- 2 large egg whites
- 16 ounces frozen strawberries, slightly thawed
- 3/4 cup sugar
- 8 ounces whipped topping
- 1 teaspoon vanilla
- For the crust:
- 1 tablespoon butter
- 8 tablespoons butter, melted
- 3 cups graham cracker crumbs (about 18 whole graham crackers) *Use gluten free if needed
- 1 tablespoon water, or more if needed

Direction

- Use the 1 Tablespoon of butter to grease 2 9 inch pie pans.
- In a small bowl combine melted butter and graham cracker crumbs. Stir until crumbs start to adhere to each other. If needed, add water by the Tablespoon until crumbs are cohesive. Divide the mixture between the two pans and use your fingers to press it onto the bottom and up the sides of the pan.
- For the filling, place egg whites, strawberries, and sugar in the bowl of an electric mixer fitted with the whisk attachment. Beat mixture for 15 minutes or until puffed and fluffy. Gently stir in whipped topping and vanilla. Divide mixture evenly between two pans. Wrap tightly with saran wrap then foil and freeze for at least 24 hours or up to 3 months.
- To serve, place the bottom of the pan in extra hot water for about 5 minutes to loosen the crust. Then slice and serve with chocolate syrup, sliced strawberries, and whipped cream, if desired.

49. Green Mojito Smoothie

Serving: Serves 2 | Prep: | Cook: | Ready in:

Ingredients

- For the smoothie:
- 1 cup (240 milliliters) coconut water or water
- 1 teaspoon finely grated lime zest
- 2 limes, peeled and quartered
- 1 cup (25 grams) torn-up curly green kale leaves (1 or 2 large leaves with stalk removed)

- 1/2 cup (18 grams) firmly packed mint
- 2 cups (320 grams) frozen pineapple
- 5 drops alcohol-free liquid stevia, plus more to taste
- Optional boosters:
- 1 teaspoon wheatgrass powder
- 1 teaspoon minced ginger
- 1 teaspoon coconut oil

Direction

- Throw all of the ingredients into your blender and blast on high for 30 to 60 seconds, until smooth and creamy.

50. Grilled Apricot Ice Cream

Serving: Makes 2 quarts | Prep: 2hours0mins | Cook: 0hours40mins | Ready in:

Ingredients

- 1 pound apricots
- 1 tablespoon olive oil
- 1/2 cup egg whites
- 1/2 cup granulated sugar
- 1/4 cup dark brown sugar
- 2 1/2 cups heavy cream

Direction

- Wash and dry apricots. Cut in half. Brush cut sides with olive oil.
- Place cut side down on hot grill surface. Cook until edges just begin to bubble and slight caramelization occurs. Flip and cook uncut surfaces until fruit edges are softened.
- Cut grilled apricots into ½" chunks and set aside to cool.
- Whisk egg white in bowl over hot water. When thoroughly aerated, slowly add sugars in a continuous stream while continuing to whisk. Continue whisking whites and sugars until hot - 120 degrees Fahrenheit. Remove from heat and beat until soft peaks form.

- Allow to cool further. Beat in cream 2 tbsps. at a time for the first cup, then ¼ cup at a time. Don't worry about the mixture being very fluid, you are not trying to make buttercream here. Cover and chill.
- Add cooled cream mix and apricots to ice cream maker and process.
- Remove from ice cream maker and transfer to sealed containers and freeze until firm. Best if allowed to sit out of the freezer for 5 minutes before serving.

51. Homemade Thandai

Serving: Serves 3 | Prep: 0hours15mins | Cook: 0hours10mins | Ready in:

Ingredients

- 3 tablespoon sugar
- Saffron a pinch
- 3 tablespoon milk (for saffron)
- Thandai Ingredients to grind:
- 15 Almonds
- 15 Cashewnuts
- 1 teaspoon poppy seeds
- 1teaspoon fennel seeds
- 1/2 teaspoon peppercorns
- 5 cardamom
- 1 teaspoon watermelon seeds
- 1 teaspoon rose essence
- To decorate:
- 1 tablespoon chopped pistachios
- 1 tablespoon chopped almonds

Direction

- Soak all the thandai paste ingredients in hot water for 10 to 15 minutes.
- While the thandai paste ingredients are soaked up, Heat milk in a saucepan, add sugar. Stir till the sugar dissolves completely and bring to boil and turn off the heat and set aside.
- Take some spoonful of boiled milk and pour into the bowl that has saffron. Set aside.

- Now, Pour the soaked thandai ingredients into a blender and grind to a paste.
- Add the ground thandai paste to the boiled milk and pour in half of the saffron milk. Give a stir, the milk looks like a pale yellow color. Keep the milk aside for 20 minutes. Or you can refrigerate to get a chilled milk.
- After the thandai paste is steeped in milk for good 20 minutes, sieve the milk using a fine mesher.
- Thandai milk is ready! Then add remaining saffron milk, chopped nuts, rose essence. Give a stir.
- Keep in the freezer for 10 to 15 minutes and then serve.
- NOTES
- Use whole milk that is not skimmed so that your drink is delicious with a thick, creamy texture.
- Let the mixture sit for an hour so that all the flavors are infused in it before boiling.
- Prepare this drink in advance because it tastes best when served chilled.
- Use a fine sieve to strain the mixture so that the residue of the ground dry fruits does not ruin the texture of the smooth drink.
- If you want a creamy texture, you can also soak the ingredients such as almond and cashew overnight so that it is soft while grinding.

52. Honey Dew Basil Ice Pops

Serving: Makes 6 | Prep: | Cook: | Ready in:

Ingredients

- 1 cup honeydew, cubed
- 1/4 cup fresh basil leaves, chopped coarsely

Direction

- 1. Add honeydew melon and basil to blender and blend until smooth.

- 2. Pour into ice-pop mold and freeze for 24 hours. To remove pops from mold, place under warm water until stick can easily be pulled out.

53. Hoodsie Cups

Serving: Makes 8 hoodsie cups | Prep: | Cook: | Ready in:

Ingredients

- For the vanilla ice cream:
- 1 cup whole milk
- 1 cup heavy cream
- 1 tablespoon vanilla extract
- 6 egg yolks
- 1/2 cup granulated sugar
- 1/2 teaspoon sea salt
- For the chocolate ice cream:
- 1 cup whole milk
- 1 cup heavy cream
- 1 tablespoon vanilla extract
- 1/2 cup unsweetened cocoa powder
- 6 egg yolks
- 1/2 cup granulated sugar
- 1/2 teaspoon sea salt

Direction

- For the vanilla ice cream:
- Begin by preparing the vanilla ice cream. In a saucepan over medium heat, add the milk, cream, and vanilla. Bring the liquid to a gentle simmer, uncovered. Remove the mixture from the heat and set it aside.
- In a separate bowl, vigorously whisk the yolks, sugar, and salt together. Slowly pour half of the warm cream mixture into the yolks while whisking.
- Pour the egg, sugar, and cream mixture into the saucepan and return to medium-low heat. Stir it in a figure-eight motion with a wooden spoon or rubber spatula for several minutes, until the mixture has slightly thickened.

- Remove the pan from the heat. Pour the mixture into a heatproof bowl and press plastic wrap directly against the liquid to prevent a skin from forming.
- Place it into the refrigerator to chill until very cold, about 2 hours. At this point, you can start on the chocolate ice cream. At this point, you can start on the chocolate ice cream (see recipe below).
- For the chocolate ice cream:
- The chocolate ice cream follows almost the same procedure as the vanilla ice cream, but (you guessed it) with cocoa powder. To make it, add the milk, cream, vanilla, and cocoa powder to a saucepan over medium heat.
- Repeat the same method you followed for the vanilla custard, and place it in the refrigerator to chill for 2 hours.
- Meanwhile, prepare your paper cups. Fold a large piece of aluminum foil, about 1 square foot, into itself until you have a small rectangle that will fit across the middle your paper cup. It should be short and thick, and strong enough to hold back a wall of ice cream. Take another smaller piece of aluminum foil and crumple it into a ball that can be stuffed into one side of the paper cup so that there is enough resistance when you fill the other side with ice cream.
- Once the vanilla custard has been chilled, churn the vanilla ice cream in an ice cream maker according to the manufacturers' instructions until it has reached a soft-serve consistency.
- Once the custard has been churned, spoon it into a piping bag fitted with a large nozzle. Evenly distribute the vanilla ice cream, piping it into one side of each paper cup, being sure to only fill one side. Cover each paper cup with a bit of plastic wrap and place in the freezer. Allow the vanilla ice cream to freeze until solid, 6 hours or up to overnight.
- Once the vanilla ice cream is fully frozen, churn the chocolate ice cream in your ice cream machine according to the manufacturers' instructions. Once the ice cream has been churned to a soft-serve consistency, spoon it into a piping bag fitted with a large nozzle.
- Take the half-vanilla cups out of the freezer and remove the aluminum foil from the center, leaving only the solid half of vanilla ice cream in the cups. Pipe the chocolate ice cream into the empty side, next to the solid vanilla ice cream.
- Cover each paper cup with a bit of plastic wrap and return to the freezer. Allow them to freeze until solid, six hours or up to overnight.
- Remove them from the freezer and enjoy them on the beach, at the park, on a boat, or at the game!

54. Irish Car Bomb Float

Serving: Serves 1 | Prep: | Cook: |Ready in:

Ingredients

- 1.5 ounces Irish whiskey (preferably Jameson)
- 4 ounces Irish Cream ice cream (I used Ben and Jerry's Dublin Mudslide but Haagen Dazs Baileys Irish Cream would be good, too)
- 12 ounces Guinness beer (or any other stout beer)

Direction

- Pour the whiskey into a pint glass.
- Add the ice cream to the glass.
- Slowly pour the Guinness over the ice cream, making sure that a head forms. Serve immediately.

55. Key Lime Pie Popsicles

Serving: Makes 10 | Prep: | Cook: |Ready in:

Ingredients

- 1 14 oz can sweetened condensed milk

- 3/4 cup Plain greek yogurt
- 3/4 cup Water
- 1/2 cup Fresh lime juice (or even better, key lime juice!)
- 2 Graham Crackers

Direction

- Mix together the sweetened condensed milk, yogurt, water, and lime juice and pour into your Popsicle mold. Cover and freeze for about 1 hour so they are just beginning to set, then insert the Popsicle sticks (this will ensure Popsicle sticks stick straight into the pops, rather than floating at an angle). Freeze until firm - I like to let these set at least 8 hours if you can wait that long.
- Finely crush graham crackers (I find that the trusty Ziploc bag and rolling pin method works great for this), and pour into a shallow dish.
- Remove Popsicle mold from freezer and run hot water over the bottom of the molds for 20-30 seconds to loosen pops. Remove pops from molds and roll in crushed graham crackers to coat. Popsicles can be served immediately or individually wrapped in parchment paper and stored in the freezer for several days.

56. Lemon Pudding Cake

Serving: Serves 3 | Prep: 0hours20mins | Cook: 0hours10mins | Ready in:

Ingredients

- All purpose flour- 1/2 cup
- Butter- 1/4 cup (melted)
- lemon zest- 1 tbs
- lemon juice- 2 tbs
- white sugar- 1 cup + 2 tbs
- baking powder- 1/2 tsp
- eggs- 2 (seperated)
- milk- 1 cup
- salt- to taste

Direction

- Mix the butter, lemon zest, lemon juice, sugar, flour, baking powder, salt in a bowl.
- Stir in the milk and mix well, then add egg yolks and mix quickly.
- Whip the egg whites until the soft peaks in medium speed.
- Fold the whipped egg whites into the batter.
- Pour the mixture into the ramekins
- Bake in the preheated oven for 350*F (or) 175*C for 30 mins.
- Allow to cool before serving!

57. Lemon Verbena Ice Cream

Serving: Makes four cups | Prep: | Cook: |Ready in:

Ingredients

- 1 cup Gently packed lemon verbena leaves
- 3/4 cup sugar
- 2 1/2 cups whole milk
- 1 1/4 cups whipping cream

Direction

- Process the lemon verbena leaves and the sugar in a food processor until very finely ground.
- In a bowl, combine the lemon verbena sugar with the milk and cream and stir until it's completely dissolved. Strain the mixture through a fine sieve.
- Pour the mixture into an ice cream maker and follow the manufacturer's directions. Enjoy!

58. Lemon Basil Sorbet

Serving: Makes 3 cups | Prep: | Cook: |Ready in:

Ingredients

- 2 1/2 cups water
- 2 cups granulated sugar
- 3 lemons, rind peeled into long strips
- 1 cup packed fresh basil leaves
- 5 tablespoons fresh lemon juice

Direction

- In a small saucepan, combine water, sugar and lemon rind. Bring to a boil over high, stirring with a wooden spoon until sugar dissolves. Remove from heat; add basil leaves. Set aside until cool, about 30 minutes. Strain lemon-basil syrup; discard solids. Stir in lemon juice. Pour syrup into an ice cream maker; freeze according to manufacturer's instructions.

59. Li Hing Mui Apple Ice Cream

Serving: Makes 1 quart | Prep: | Cook: | Ready in:

Ingredients

- 2 cups whole milk
- 1 1/4 cups heavy cream
- 2/3 cup sugar
- 2 tablespoons light corn syrup
- 1 1/2 tablespoons cornstarch
- 3 tablespoons cream cheese
- 1/8 teaspoon sea salt
- 1 fuji apple
- 1/3 cup li hing mui powder

Direction

- Freeze bowl: Approximately 18 hours ahead of time: Place the ice cream bowl in the freezer. Make sure the freezer is set to 0 degrees or colder.
- Prep apples: Finely dice the apple into small pieces. (About the size of a tic-tac) Bake at 350 for 10-12 minutes until it is soft to the touch. Set aside to cool.
- Prep for the ice cream base: Mix about 2 tablespoons of the milk with the cornstarch in

a small bowl to make a smooth slurry. Whisk the cream cheese and salt in a medium bowl until smooth. Fill a large bowl with ice and water.

- Cook: Combine the remaining milk, the cream, sugar, corn syrup in a 4-quart saucepan, bring to a rolling boil over medium-high heat, and boil for 4 minutes -- watch it closely and stir occasionally to make sure it doesn't boil over.
- Thicken: Gradually whisk the cornstarch slurry into the strained mixture. Bring the mixture back to a boil over medium-high heat and cook, stirring with a heatproof spatula, until slightly thickened, about 1 minute. Remove from the heat.
- Chill: Gradually whisk the hot milk mixture into the cream cheese until smooth. Pour the mixture into a 1-gallon Ziploc freezer bag and submerge the sealed bag in the ice bath. Place in fridge for 30 minutes to an hour until cold.
- Freeze: Pour the ice cream mixture into the frozen canister and turn on the machine. Add the li hing mui powder into the bowl while it is mixing. Spin the ice cream until thick and creamy. Once it reaches the desired consistency, gently mix in the apple pieces.
- Pack the ice cream into a storage container, and seal with an airtight lid. Freeze in the coldest part of your freezer until firm, about 4 hours.

60. London Fog Popsicles

Serving: Makes 8 | Prep: | Cook: | Ready in:

Ingredients

- 1 1/2 cups just boiled water from the kettle
- 2 Earl Grey tea bags
- 1 teaspoon vanilla extract
- 1 tablespoon sugar
- 1 1/2 cups whole milk

Direction

- Place tea bags in a large jug or container. Pour in 1 1/2 cups hot water and let steep, 10 minutes. Stir in vanilla extract and sugar. Mix in the whole milk.
- Divide mixture between 8 popsicle molds. Secure popsicle sticks with clothespins, or let mixture freeze until slushy, about 1 hour, before adding popsicle sticks. Let popsicles freeze completely, about 2 hours. Briefly run warm water under the molds before removing popsicles.

61. Made With Ferrero Rocher Nutella Ice Cream

Serving: Serves 3 | Prep: | Cook: |Ready in:

Ingredients

- 200 milliliters whole milk
- 200 milliliters heavy cream
- 80 grams sugar
- 1 pinch salt
- 3 teaspoons cornstarch
- 50 grams cream cheese
- 150 grams nutella
- 5 Ferrero Rocher candies

Direction

- Dissolve the cornstarch in 50ml whole milk, leave to rest.
- In a small saucepan combine the heavy cream, the leftover milk, the sugar and a pinch salt, place on medium, bring to an almost boil, add the cornstarch milk and cook constantly stirring until thickened. Take off heat, add the cream cheese and Nutella, mix until smooth and combined. Cool to room temperature, then transfer to the fridge overnight.
- Freeze in your ice cream maker according to the manufacturer's instructions, adding quartered Ferrero Roche candies at the last couple of minutes of churning. Store in an airtight container in the freezer or spoon right away.
- Pair with hazelnut and chocolate ice creams.

62. Mango Habanero Yogurt

Serving: Serves 4 | Prep: | Cook: |Ready in:

Ingredients

- Mango Habanero Yogurt
- 1/2 cup Mango Nectar
- 2 Habanero Peppers
- 1 1 inch cube Fresh Ginger, peeled
- 2 Mangos
- 4 Strawberries
- 1 tablespoon Lime juice (juice of 1 lime)
- 1 cup Greek Yogurt (I used Fage 0% Fat Free)
- 1/2 cup Half & Half
- 2 pinches Salt
- 2 tablespoons Vodka (optional)
- Mango Sauce
- 1 cup Mango Nectar (the rest of the can)
- 1 tablespoon Butter
- 1 teaspoon Sugar
- 1 pint Salt

Direction

- Cut the Habanero (wear latex gloves!) into pieces, discarding the stem and seeds. Scrape the peel from the ginger with the side of a spoon, and then chop into a few pieces. Add the Habanero, Ginger, and the 1/2 cup Mango Nectar into a small saucepan and bring to a simmer. Simmer gently for about 2 minutes, then remove from heat. Remove or strain out the peppers and ginger, and let cool. The nectar will reduce to about 1 1/2 Tablespoons of liquid.
- Peel and dice Mangoes and place in blender. Remove stems from Strawberries, and add to blender. Add 1 TBLS lime juice, and puree until smooth.

- Add the cooled nectar, and 2 pinches of salt to the puree in the blender. Add in the Yogurt and the Half & Half. Blend until well mixed. Chill mixture for several hours, or overnight. (If adding Vodka, stir in just prior to freezing. The Vodka will help keep the yogurt softer for a longer time.)
- Freeze following the directions for your ice cream maker.
- For sauce, use the remainder of the Mango Nectar. Heat over Medium-Low heat to a simmer. Add 1 TBLS butter, 1 tsp sugar and 1 pinch salt. Simmer for about 4-5 minutes until mixture begins to thicken. Let cool.

63. Marzipan Stollen Ice Cream

Serving: Serves 8 | Prep: | Cook: | Ready in:

Ingredients

- Base
- 1 cup Half and Half
- 2 Cinnamon Sticks, broken in half
- 1/4 teaspoon nutmeg
- 1/4 teaspoon cloves
- 1 peel from 1 large orange
- 2/3 cup sugar
- 4 egg yolks
- 3 tablespoons honey
- 2 cups heavy cream
- Mix-Ins
- 1 cup chopped dried fruit such as raisins, currants, cherries, blueberries, and cranberries
- 1 cup marzipan, cut into half inch cubes
- 1/4 cup candied orange peel cut into tiny bits (~1/8 inch cubes)
- brandy

Direction

- In a bowl place dried fruit and add just enough brandy to cover the fruit. Place in fridge, covered to soak until hydrated.
- Place the marzipan bits in the freezer separated on a cookie sheet to get cold overnight.
- Warm the half and half, sugar, spices, and orange peel in a small saucepan until the sugar dissolves. Remove from heat and allow to steep for 30 min.
- Place the cream in a large bowl and place a thin mesh strainer over the cream.
- Rewarm the half and half/sugar/spice mixture over low heat. In another bowl, whisk the yolks. When the mixture is warm, add some of the mixture to the yolks, slowly, while whisking constantly in order to temper the yolks.
- Scrape all the yolk mixture back into the saucepan.
- Heat the mixture gently, constantly whisking, until the custard thickens and coats the back of a spoon.
- Pour the mixture through the strainer and into the cream. Discard any spice bits, orange peel, or gunk that remains.
- Warm the honey (I used the microwave for about 15-20 seconds) and then stir it into the rest of the custard base.
- Chill the base in the refrigerator overnight.
- The next day, churn the ice cream base as per the instructions of your machine.
- While churning, strain off any excess brandy from the fruit. Press gently to get any that have over-soaked. (Feel free to drink your now delicious flavored brandy!)
- When churned, place about 1/4 of the ice cream in a wide container and spread evenly. Sprinkle 1/3 of the brandied fruit, marzipan chunks, and candied orange.
- Add another 1/4 of the ice cream and repeat the layering process. Try not to move the fruit too much or the color will bleed.
- In the end you should have 4 layers of ice cream base + 3 layers of fillings in between.
- Place a piece of wax paper over the surface to prevent freezer burn, place the container lid tightly, and freeze overnight. Enjoy!

64. Max Falkowitz' Best (and Easiest) Frozen Yogurt Recipe

Serving: Makes 1 quart | Prep: | Cook: |Ready in:

Ingredients

- 1 quart container (about 3 3/4 cups) full-fat plain yogurt (see note above about substituting for Greek)
- 1 cup sugar
- 1/4 teaspoon kosher salt

Direction

- Whisk yogurt, sugar, and salt together in a mixing bowl until sugar has completely dissolved. Chill in an ice bath or refrigerate until yogurt registers at least 45°F on an instant-read thermometer (i.e. thoroughly chilled — this is roughly fridge temperature).
- Churn yogurt in ice cream machine according to manufacturer's instructions. Scoop and eat like soft serve, or transfer ice cream to airtight container and chill in freezer for at least 4 to 5 hours before serving.

65. Mint Avocado Chip Ice Cream Sandwiches

Serving: Makes 12 | Prep: | Cook: |Ready in:

Ingredients

- Chocolate Sandwich Cookies
- 233 grams butter, room temp
- 177 grams sugar
- 2 egg yolks
- 1 teaspoon vanilla extract
- 300 grams all purpose flour
- 33 grams black cocoa powder (can sub regular)
- .5 teaspoons salt

- Mint Avocado Ice Cream
- 464 grams avocado
- .5 cups mint leaves
- 2 cups milk
- 1.5 cups heavy cream
- 300 grams sugar
- 1 pinch salt

Direction

- Chocolate Sandwich Cookies
- Cream butter with sugar, 2-3 minutes.
- Add yolks and vanilla. Beat to combine.
- Whisk together dry ingredients.
- Add dry ingredients to butter, sugar and eggs. Stir until combined.
- Roll dough between two sheets of parchment until 1/4" thick.
- Refrigerate dough at least 2 hours.
- Cut dough into 2.5" circles.
- Bake cookies at 325 degrees F for 8-10 minutes.
- Mint Avocado Ice Cream
- Bring milk, cream, and mint to a simmer and then steep off the heat for 1 hour.
- Strain out mint leaves from milk and cream.
- In a blender, blend all ingredients.
- Freeze ice cream in an ice cream maker.
- Sandwich chocolate cookies with avocado ice cream and roll edges in chocolate chips.
- Freeze sandwiches until solid, approximately 1-2 hours.

66. Mint Chocolate Sorbet

Serving: Makes 1 quart | Prep: | Cook: |Ready in:

Ingredients

- 2 1/4 cups water
- 3/4 cup sugar
- 1/4 cup glucose syrup or corn syrup
- 1 cup packed mint leaves (approximate)
- 3/4 cup unsweetened cocoa powder (preferably Dutch processed, but natural works too)

- 1/4 teaspoon kosher salt
- 6 ounces semisweet or bittersweet chocolate, chopped
- 1/4 teaspoon vanilla extract

Direction

- In a medium saucepan add the sugar and the mint leaves. Gently press the mint leaves into the sugar to help extract the oils. Add 1 1/2 cups (375 ml) of the water and all of the glucose or corn syrup and salt. Bring to a boil, stirring frequently, until the sugar is dissolved. Remove from heat, cover, and let steep for about 20 minutes. Strain out the mint leaves and discard.
- Return the mint syrup mixture to the saucepan, add the cocoa powder, and whisk to combine. Bring to a boil, stirring frequently. Once it reaches a boil, keep it boiling for about 1 minute, stirring all the while. Remove from heat.
- Place the chocolate pieces in a heat proof bowl. Pour the mint and cocoa mixture over the chocolate and let sit for a few minutes to melt the chocolate, then whisk until the chocolate is thoroughly melted and mixed in.
- Stir in the remaining 3/4 cup (180 ml) water and the vanilla extract. Chill the mixture overnight (or pour the mixture into a zip top bag and submerge in an ice bath for 30 minutes), until it reaches 40°F or below. Sometimes the mixture develops a thick layer on the top as it chills overnight–just whisk it in before you add it to the ice cream maker. Process in an ice cream maker.

67. Mocha Chip Ice Cream

Serving: Makes 1 quart | Prep: | Cook: | Ready in:

Ingredients

- 2 cups Heavy Cream
- 1/2 cup 1/2 and 1/2

- 1/2 cup Whole Milk
- 1/2 cup sugar plus 1 Tablesoon
- 2 tablespoons Ground espresso or dark coffee grounds
- 1 tablespoon Baking Powder
- 1 tablespoon Vanilla
- 3 Egg Yolks
- 1-4 ounces Dark Chocolate bar (Ghirardelli or better)

Direction

- Place cream, 1/2 and 1/2, milk and egg yolks in saucepan on medium low.
- Measure sugar, espresso, baking powder and pour in saucepan with milk. Whisk continually until all of sugar has dissolved and eggs are well incorporated.
- Once milk mixture is done, add vanilla and remove from heat. Place in ice cream maker and follow manufacturer's directions.
- While ice cream is being made, chop dark chocolate into bite size pieces. When ice cream is almost complete add chocolate to ice cream mix. Mix chocolate in.

68. No Bake Sugar Free Chocolate Bars

Serving: Serves 5 | Prep: | Cook: | Ready in:

Ingredients

- Pecan Date Dough
- 1 cup Raw Peacans
- 1 cup Pitted Soft Dates
- Melted Chocolate Topping
- 1/4 cup Unsweetened Cocoa Powder
- 1 tablespoon Maple Syrup
- 1 tablespoon Coconut Oil, melted

Direction

- Place pecans & dates in a food processor & pulse until it forms a coarse meal-like texture.

- Pulse for a few more seconds until it the dough clumps together.
- Place the mixture on parchment paper and press to flatten into 1/2 inch thick rectangle.
- In a small mixing bowl, combine melted coconut oil, cocoa powder, & honey or maple syrup and mix until smooth. The mixture should resemble thick melted chocolate.
- Pour the chocolate mixture over the date and pecan dough and freeze for about an hour.
- Cut in individual portions and store in the freezer.

69. Orange Milk Sherbet

Serving: Serves 10 | Prep: | Cook: | Ready in:

Ingredients

- 1 1/2 cups sugar
- 1 1/2 teaspoons orange zest
- 1/4 cup lemon juice
- 1 1/2 cups orange juice
- 4 cups cold milk

Direction

- Combine the chopped zest and the sugar.
- Whisk the lemon and orange juice into the sugar until the sugar has completely dissolved.
- Gradually stir in the milk. If the milk curdles slightly, it will not affect the texture after the sherbet is frozen.
- Freeze in the ice cream maker of your choice!

70. Orange Panna Cotta With Cardamom Honey

Serving: Serves 6 | Prep: | Cook: | Ready in:

Ingredients

- 1 & 1/2 cups Heavy Cream
- 12 ounces evaporated milk
- 3/4 cup Sugar
- 4 package powdered gelatin
- 1 teaspoon Salt
- 1/2 Vanilla Bean , Split
- 1 cup Orange Juice
- Zest of 2 orange
- 4 tablespoons Honey
- 1 teaspoon Cardamom Powder

Direction

- Take 4 ounces of evaporated milk and gelatin and let it bloom for few minutes at least 5 to 6 minutes. In a saucepan, take evaporated milk and heavy cream bring it to boil. Scrap out the vanilla add it to the boiling milk, add sugar, salt and orange zest. Mix well.
- Once the milk mixture is simmered enough, add it to the gelatin mixture and mix it well. Add the orange juice to this and mix. Remove it into individual bowls. Refrigerate it for more than 3 hours preferably overnight.
- Mix powdered cardamom with honey. Unmold the Panna Cotta on a plate, drizzle it with cardamom infused honey. Garnish it with mint leaves. For unmolding the Panna Cotta, I keep it in warm water for 2 minutes and run down a knife at the sides.

71. Orange Vanilla Coconut Milk Ice Cream

Serving: Serves 1 - 2 | Prep: | Cook: | Ready in:

Ingredients

- Ice Cream
- 1 14 oz can organic full fat coconut milk or make your own, recipe below
- 25 drops Vanilla Sweetleaf liquid stevia
- 1 teaspoon Orange extract
- 1/2 teaspoon Orange flower water (optional)
- Coconut Milk

- 1 part shredded coconut
- 2 parts warm filtered water

Direction

- If using homemade coconut milk make your milk. Put 1 part shredded coconut and 2 parts warm water in a blender. For this recipe use 1 cup of coconut and 2 cups of warm filtered water.
- Blend the coconut and water for 1 - 2 minutes. Strain the coconut from the water with a sieve or a straining bag used for nut milk and reserve the water. You can do this twice if you like, but the second batch will be less creamy.
- In a bowl mix the coconut milk, vanilla stevia, orange extract and orange flower water if using with a whisk until well incorporated. Taste. Adjust.
- Pour mixed ingredients into a quart Ziploc bag. Place bag flat in freezer preferably between two Ziploc bags filled with ice and salt or any ice packs.
- It should be ready in 15 to 20 minutes. Squeeze the bag to soften it up and cut off a corner to squeeze it out into small bowls for soft serve or if it gets too hard throw it in a blender or food processor and serve. Blend with some soda water for a milkshake.

72. Orange, Anise Seed And Honey Greek Yogurt Pops

Serving: Makes 8 - 10 depending on the size of your mold | Prep: | Cook: |Ready in:

Ingredients

- ¼ cup wildflower honey
- 1 teaspoon anise seeds, finely crushed using a mortar and pestle
- ¼ cup orange juice concentrate (See note below.)
- 1 1/2 cups full fat Greek yogurt
- ½ cup almond milk (or regular milk)

- 2 tiny drops almond extract

Direction

- Warm the honey in the microwave for about 30 seconds. (I do this in a one cup glass measure.) Add the anise seeds and allow to cool and infuse. If you don't want the seeds in your pops, heat the honey again and strain the seeds.
- In a medium bowl, whisk together all of the ingredients until thoroughly blended. Put into frozen pop molds. Freeze until hard.
- Enjoy! ;o)
- NB Orange juice concentrate is amazing stuff. Did you know that it's largely composed of peels, of a variety of orange or combinations of oranges selected to give the fullest taste? John McPhee wrote a fascinating series of long reads for the New Yorker about this years ago. I am fairly certain that they were brought together into a book. In any event, I love using the stuff when I need a good boost of natural orange flavor. ;o)

73. Orange Scented Smoked Tea Ice Cream

Serving: Makes 1 tub | Prep: | Cook: |Ready in:

Ingredients

- 1 1/2 cups whole milk
- 1 1/2 cups cream
- 1 large orange
- 2 teaspoons lapsang souchong tea (or 2 tea bags)
- 1 cup sugar
- 1 teaspoon vanilla
- 9 large egg yolks
- 1 pinch salt
- 3 tablespoons cassis

Direction

- Use a peeler to peel orange being careful to not get any pith. If necessary, use a sharp knife to remove any. Chiffonade 2 T and set aside. Place the rest of zest in a pot with milk, cream and tea bags and heat to a gentle simmer for a minute. Turn off heat and steep for 15 minutes. Mixture should have a subtle, smokey tea flavor. Strain and return to pot.
- Fill a large bowl with ice water and place a second bowl inside. Have a strainer ready.
- Whisk egg yolks with 3/4 c sugar until slightly thickened and paler in color. Heat milk mixture to simmer again and add a bit to eggs whisking briskly. Return all to pot and simmer, whisking, until it begins to thicken. It should be pourable, but still coat the back of a spoon.
- Pour custard through strainer into bowl in ice and stir until mixture is cool. Stir in cassis and salt, adjusting for taste. Place mixture in fridge until cold, then churn in ice cream maker according to instructions.
- Heat remaining 1/4 sugar with 1/4 cup water and simmer remaining zest for 5 minutes. Drain, spread out on wax paper and allow to try. Toss with a bit of sugar. When ice cream is done, fold zest in, pack into containers and chill in freezer until ready to eat.

74. Oreo Dessert

Serving: Serves a crowd | Prep: 2hours0mins | Cook: 0hours6mins | Ready in:

Ingredients

- 24 Oreo cookies (272 grams) (the classic kind, not double-stuff)
- 1 1/2 sticks (12 tablespoons, 170 grams) salted butter, divided, plus more for pan (use salted; it makes a big difference!)
- 1/2 gallon (2 quarts) of your favorite vanilla ice cream
- 4 ounces (113 grams) German's sweet chocolate (such as Baker's brand)
- 2/3 cup (135 grams) granulated sugar
- 1 small can evaporated milk (5 fluid ounces, 147 mL)

Direction

- For crust: Butter the bottom of a 9x13x2 pan (such as Pyrex). Melt 1/2 stick butter (4 tablespoons) in a bowl. Crush the Oreo cookies into fine crumbs with a little texture. (For ease, place the cookies in a zipper-lock bag, seal, and then crush with a rolling pin. Turn the bag inside-out to scrape out all of the crumbs.) Mix the Oreo crumbs with the melted butter in the pan, and press them evenly into the bottom. Cover the pan and freeze until the crust is set, about 30 minutes.
- For filling: Let the ice cream soften a bit on the counter until it's spreadable. Evenly spread it over the Oreo crust. Cover the pan and return to the freezer for at least an hour to set the ice cream.
- For fudge topping: Combine the remaining stick of butter (8 tablespoons), chocolate, sugar, and evaporated milk in a saucepan. Bring to a low boil and cook for 4 minutes, stirring constantly. Cool to room temperature. (If in a hurry, set the saucepan in an ice bath to speed up the cooling process, stirring several times and scraping down the sides of the bowl. It should be ready in 5 to 10 minutes.) Working quickly, pour the fudge evenly over the ice cream, covering as much as possible, then spread with a knife to distribute the fudge in a smooth, even layer. Cover the pan and return to the freezer for another hour or two, or until fully frozen and set.
- When ready to serve, let the Oreo dessert sit on the counter for about 5 minutes to take the chill off (and make cutting easier), then cut into squares and serve. Tightly covered, it'll keep well in the freezer for several weeks.

75. Pistachio Raspberry Gelato Sorbetto Cake

Serving: Serves so many | Prep: | Cook: |Ready in:

Ingredients

- 1 cup plus 2 tablespoons (145 grams) pistachios
- 1 teaspoon lemon zest
- 1/2 cup (67 grams) all-purpose flour
- 1/2 stick (57 grams) unsalted butter, cubed and chilled
- 1/4 cup (75 grams) raspberry jam
- 1/2 teaspoon rose water (optional)
- 2 pints pistachio gelato, divided
- 2 pints raspberry sorbetto, divided
- 1 cup frozen raspberries

Direction

- To prepare the pistachios and the crumble, heat the oven to 375F/190C. Move the pistachios to the bowl of a food processor; pulse 30 times. Remove one quarter of the pistachios from the processor, and set them aside. To the food processor, add the lemon zest, flour, and sugar; pulse 10 more times. Add the butter, and mix until everything just comes together, about 1 minute. Empty the pistachio shortbread onto a baking sheet; use your fingers to crumble and separate the "dough," so that it is spread out across the baking sheet, and is not too clumpy. Bake for 20 minutes, or until the shortbread crumbles are golden and aromatic. Allow the crumbles to cool completely, at least 30 minutes.
- To make the raspberry drizzle, spoon the jam into a small bowl. Add 1 tablespoon water, and the rosewater is using, and stir until completely incorporated. Refrigerate until needed.
- To begin the gelato/sorbetto cake, pack one third of the pistachio crumbles into the bottom of a 6-inch springform pan. Using a large spoon, add 1 pint of the pistachio gelato to the springform; use the back of the spoon to smooth the top. Add another third of the crumbles, and then repeat with 1 pint of the raspberry the sorbetto. Over the sorbetto, scatter 1/2 cup of the frozen raspberries and 1/2 the raspberry drizzle. Finish with the remaining pistachio crumbles. Cover with plastic wrap, and move the springform to the freezer for at least 2 hours, but up to overnight.
- To finish the gelato/sorbetto cake, prepare a warm glass of water and an ice cream scoop. Working quickly, and alternating between the remaining pint of pistachio gelato and raspberry sorbetto, "decorate" the top of the cake with fat scoops. Drape the plastic back over the cake, and move it back to the freezer for another 3 hours, or up to overnight.
- To serve the gelato/sorbetto cake, remove the cake from the freezer. Undo the springform, so that the cake stands alone. Decorate the top with the remaining raspberry drizzle, crushed pistachios, and remaining frozen raspberries. Slice and serve right away.

76. Piña Colada Coconut Green Smoothie

Serving: Serves 1 | Prep: | Cook: |Ready in:

Ingredients

- 3/4 cup Lecroix coconut water
- 2 teaspoons Chia seeds
- 1 Protein powder - low sugar, vanilla, 1 serving per package directions
- 2 cups Frozen or fresh torn kale or spinach
- 1 cup Frozen pineapple chunks
- 3 tablespoons Canned coconut cream
- 1/2 cup Ice cubes

Direction

- Place all ingredients in a blender in order listed above, and blend until completely smooth.

77. Plum Sorbet

Serving: Serves 3 | Prep: | Cook: |Ready in:

Ingredients

- 550 grams ripe pitted plums
- 130 grams sugar
- 3 tablespoons lemon juice
- 1 pinch salt
- 70 milliliters water

Direction

- In a small saucepan over medium heat combine the halved and pitted ripe plums (keep the skins), water, lemon juice, sugar and a pinch of salt, cook 15min until the plums are soft and the syrup gets tinted deep red from the plum skins. Take off heat, cool slightly. Purée the mixture in a blender, then strain through a fine mesh sieve for a glossy smooth texture. Chill in the fridge overnight.
- Freeze in your ice cream maker according to the manufacturer's instructions, store in the freezer for at least 4 hours until set or spoon right away.

78. Pomegranate Molasses And Date Ice Cream

Serving: Makes 1 pint | Prep: | Cook: |Ready in:

Ingredients

- Ice cream base
- 1 cup whole milk
- 2 teaspoons corn starch
- 3/4 ounce cream cheese, at room temperature
- 1 pinch fine sea salt
- 5/8 cup heavy cream (1/2 cup + 2 tbsp)
- 1/3 cup white sugar
- 1 tablespoon light corn syrup
- Pomegranate molasses date sauce
- 20 large mejdool dates, pitted
- 1 cup hot water
- 2 tablespoons pomegranate molasses
- 1/4 cup honey
- 1 pinch fine sea salt
- 2 tablespoons corn starch
- 2 tablespoons water

Direction

- Ice cream base
- In a small bowl, mix the corn starch with 1 tbsp. of whole milk. Set aside. In another medium sized glass bowl, whisk the salt and cream cheese together. Set aside. In a big bowl, make an ice bath with lots of ice. Set aside.
- In a heavy bottomed pan, heat the rest of the milk, heavy cream, white sugar and light corn syrup. Bring to a boil and remember to stir constantly! Let it boil for 4 minutes and then switch off the heat and add the corn starch slurry, whisking constantly.
- Transfer the hot milk and cream mixture to the cream cheese mixture, adding a little at a time and whisking thoroughly to get rid of any lumps. Once the mixture is completely smooth, nestle the glass bowl in the ice-bath and let it get cold.
- Pour the cold mixture into the ice cream machine and let it run for 25 minutes.
- Pomegranate molasses date sauce
- Place the pitted dates and the hot water in a food processor and blend until very, very smooth. Pass the mixture through a fine mesh sieve lined with cheesecloth to get rid of as much of the grit as possible.
- On medium heat, in a heavy bottomed deep sauce pan, add the date mixture, pomegranate molasses, honey and salt. Stir the mixture continuously for a couple of minutes, as the minute you stop stirring it is going to hiss and splutter!
- Add the corn starch and 2 tbsp. of water together to form a smooth slurry. Add the slurry to the date mixture and continue to

- keep stirring constantly for a couple more minutes.
- Once most of the moisture has evaporated and it has thickened nicely, take it off the heat and chill in the fridge until it has cooled completely.
- Once the ice cream base has churned for 25 minutes, add the 1 cup of the cooled date mixture and let it churn for another 5 minutes. Reserve the rest of the sauce for garnish. Make sure that the sauce gets evenly distributed throughout the ice cream. Store in an airtight container and cover the surface with cling wrap. Let the ice cream ripen in the freezer overnight.
- To serve, let the ice cream sit on the counter for about 5 minutes before doling it out in big scoops. Enjoy!

79. Prince's "Raspberry SorBeret" Or Just Call It Dessert Nachos With Fruit Salsa

Serving: Serves 6 | Prep: | Cook: |Ready in:

Ingredients

- For the sorbet
- 3/4 cup water or raspberry soda (I used Hansen's)
- 1 3/4 cups sugar (1/4 c. less, if using soda)
- 1   small lemon, juiced
- 2 tablespoons raspberry liqueur (I used Chambord)
- 3 pints red raspberries
- For the Fruit Salsa and Nachos
- 12   flour tortillas
- cinnamon sprinkles (1T. each of cinnamon, sugar and 1 t. cardamon)
- 1 pint red raspberries
- 1/2 pint each of blackberries, blueberries, strawberries
- 1   white peach, diced
- 1 teaspoon each of cinnamon and cardamon
- 10   mint leaves
- 1   fresh limes, zested and juiced
- chocolate sauce for drizzling (I used my recipe from my chololate-carmel concrete)

Direction

- To make the sorbet: Boil the water (or soda) and sugar to dissolve...approx. 2 minutes to let the carbonation burn off. Cool completely and add lemon juice and liqueur.
- Puree 3 pints of raspberries in food processor, strain with a fine mesh sieve. Process according to your machine directions.
- For the fruit salsa: muddle 5 of the mint leaves with the lime juice. Add cinnamon and cardamom. Mash 1/2 of the fruit into the juice mixture
- Add rest of the fruit. Chiffonade remaining mint leaves.
- Slice tortillas into 6 pieces each. On a baking stone, lay pieces in a single layer and sprinkle water onto each one. Sprinkle cinnamon sugar mixture on top of water. Bake at 400 for 5 minutes or until golden brown.
- To prepare platter: line platter with "nacho chips". Add 3-4 scoops of raspberry sorbet, drizzle fruit salsa and chocolate sauce on top.
- Dig out your old Prince album...it's probably still in your walkman in the basement. C'mon...you know you've been humming it the whole time you've been reading!

80. Purple Sweet Potato Vanilla Bean Ice Cream

Serving: Makes a generous quart | Prep: | Cook: |Ready in:

Ingredients

- 9 ounces peeled and diced purple sweet potatoes (around 1 3/4 - 2 cups if cut into 1/2-inch cubes)
- 2 cups whole milk

- 1/2 vanilla bean, split and scraped
- 2 ounces cream cheese, softened (4 tablespoons)
- 1/4 teaspoon fine sea salt
- 1 1/4 cups heavy cream
- 2/3 cup granulated sugar
- 3 tablespoons light corn syrup

Direction

- Combine the diced sweet potatoes, milk, split vanilla bean, and scraped vanilla seeds in a saucepan and bring to a boil. Reduce the heat to low and simmer until the potatoes are soft and easily pierced with a knife -- about 10 to 12 minutes.
- Combine the cream and salt in a large bowl and beat until smooth.
- Fill a large bowl with ice and water.
- Once the potatoes are cooked, remove the split vanilla bean, then puree the mixture in the saucepan with an immersion blender (or transfer contents to a blender or food processor, blend, and return to the pan).
- Add the heavy cream, sugar, and corn syrup to the potato and milk puree. Bring the mixture to a rolling boil over medium-high heat, boil for 4 minutes, then remove from the heat. (Keep your eye on the mixture while it's boiling, if you don't pay attention, you might find it boils over quite easily.)
- Gradually whisk the hot mixture into the cream cheese and salt blend until smooth.
- Pour the mixture into a large zip-top freezer bag and submerge the sealed bag in the ice water bath until cool (adding more ice if necessary) -- this should be about 30 minutes.
- Pour the cooled mixture into the frozen canister and spin until thick and creamy.
- Grab a spoon and eat the soft-serve straight out of the frozen canister, double-dipping like no one is watching. Or, if you have restraint, put the ice cream into a freezer-safe storage container and freeze until firm. It will become very firm once frozen, so place it on the counter to warm up a bit before scooping -- the texture won't be compromised, promise!

81. Raspberry Ice Cream Sandwiches

Serving: Makes almost 2 dozen sandwiches | Prep: | Cook: | Ready in:

Ingredients

- Raspberry ice cream
- 3 cups strained raspberry puree (made from blending and straining about 30 oz. raspberries. Strain well! Frozen and defrosted raspberries work fine.)
- 1 1/2 cups heavy cream
- 1 1/2 cups half and half
- 1/2 vanilla bean
- 1 cup sugar
- 5 egg yolks
- 1 tablespoon Chambord (creme de cassis works in a pinch, but you can also skip this)
- Coconut lemon shortbread and sandwich assembly
- 1 cup unsweetened finely shredded coconut
- 1 1/2 cups unsalted butter (use good quality), soft but still slightly cooler than room temperature
- 1 cup sugar
- 1 teaspoon sea salt
- 1 teaspoon lemon juice
- the zest of 2 lemons
- 2 2/3 cups all purpose flour

Direction

- Raspberry ice cream
- In a small bowl, lightly whisk the egg yolks and set aside.
- Add the cream and half and half and sugar to a saucepan. Split the vanilla bean and scrape the insides in. Then toss in the pod, for good measure. Heat just to a simmer.
- Add about 1/4 cup of the hot liquid to the egg yolks, whisking furiously to temper the yolks. Add another 1/2 cup, continuing to whisk.

Then, scrape the egg mixture into the pot with the rest of the liquid is. Cook, stirring constantly at a low simmer until the mixture thickens to a custard consistency, thick enough to thickly coat the back of a spoon.

- Strain the custard into a bowl. Stir in the raspberry puree and Chambord until completely mixed. Refrigerate at least 4 hours (I like to leave mine overnight). Then, churn in an ice cream machine according to your machine's directions, transfer to a container and freeze.
- Use to assemble ice cream sandwiches with the cookies, as directed below.
- Coconut lemon shortbread and sandwich assembly
- Spread the coconut on a baking sheet. Bake in a 325F oven until just lightly browned, about 5 minutes. Remove from the oven and cool completely.
- In the bowl of a standing mixer fitted with the paddle attachment, cream together the butter and the sugar until light and fluffy. Then beat in the salt and lemon juice.
- Beat in the flour in two additions, adding the coconut and lemon zest with the second addition. Then beat just until the dough pulls away from the sides of the bowl and forms almost a single mass.
- Gather the dough together, flatten it into a disc, wrap it in plastic wrap and chill for at least an hour.
- Preheat your oven to 325F. On a lightly floured surface, roll the dough out to about a quarter inch thickness. Use a 2 inch round cookie cutter to cut circles. Transfer the cookies to parchment lined baking sheets.
- Gather the remaining dough together, roll it out again and cut more circles. Repeat as needed to cut all the dough (you may have some odd scraps at the end - bake them and snack on them), using as little flour as possible all the while.
- Bake the cookies for about 16-20 minutes (rotating each baking sheet halfway through the baking time), or until they are golden brown. Keep the sheets with uncooked cookies on them in the refrigerator while they wait to bake.
- Allow the cookies to cool on the baking sheet for about 3 minutes, then transfer them to a wire rack and allow them to cool completely.
- To assemble the ice cream sandwiches, let the raspberry ice cream soften slightly. Place a scoop of ice cream on top of a cookie. Top with another cookie and press down gently to make a sandwich. Wrap with plastic wrap and place in the freezer.
- Repeat until you have used up all of the cookie pairs (or all of the ice cream, whichever comes first, but they were fairly well matched). Let the sandwiches freeze until they are hardened. Then serve. They will also keep wrapped and stored in the freezer (put them in a box of some sort to protect them) for a while, just waiting for when you need them.

82. Ready To Thrive! Shamrock Shake

Serving: Makes 1 smoothie | Prep: 0hours5mins | Cook: 0hours0mins | Ready in:

Ingredients

- 1 Ready to Thrive! Green Smoothie
- 1/2 cup of plain non-fat Greek yogurt
- 1/4 cup of almond milk (or your preferred liquid base)
- 1 sliced kiwi
- 1 sprig of mint for garnish

Direction

- Dump frozen fruit from Ready to Thrive! Cup into blender
- Add plain non-fat Greek yogurt and almond milk into blender
- Blend until desired thickness
- Pour smoothie back into the reusable Ready to Thrive! Cup and garnish with sliced kiwi and mint

83. Red Velvet Cheesecake Ice Cream

Serving: Serves 3 | Prep: | Cook: |Ready in:

Ingredients

- 300 grams cream cheese
- 180 grams 20%-fat sour cream
- 125 milliliters pouring cream
- 130 grams sugar
- 1/2 teaspoon vanilla extract
- 100 grams bite-sized Red Velvet cake crumbs

Direction

- Combine the first 5 ingredients in a blender and blend until uniform, smooth and creamy. Chill in the fridge overnight.
- Freeze in your ice cream maker according to the manufacturer's instructions adding the cake crumbs at the last couple of minutes of churning. Place in an airtight container in the freezer for at least 4 hours until set.

84. Redcurrant Coconut Ice Cream

Serving: Serves 3 | Prep: | Cook: |Ready in:

Ingredients

- 400 milliliters full-fat coconut milk
- 3 teaspoons tapioca starch
- 200 grams redcurrant jelly

Direction

- Combine 100ml coconut milk with the tapioca starch, set the slurry aside.
- In a saucepan bring the leftover coconut milk to an almost boil, stir in the slurry and cook over medium heat stirring constantly until thickened. Take of heat and cool to room temperature. Transfer in the fridge to cool overnight.
- Combine the coconut custard with the preferably homemade redcurrant jelly, pour into the ice cream maker and freeze according to the manufacturer's instructions. Store in an airtight container in the freezer or spoon as a soft-serve.

85. Rhubarb Swirl Gelato

Serving: Makes 2 litres | Prep: | Cook: |Ready in:

Ingredients

- 6 cups rhubarb, sliced
- 1 cup honey
- 1/4 cup lemon juice
- 2 cans full fat coconut milk
- 2 teaspoons pure vanilla extract
- Pinch salt
- 1 tablespoon arrowroot powder

Direction

- Cook the rhubarb, honey, and lemon juice over medium heat for 8-10 minutes, or until very soft. Cool slightly and pour into your blender, mixing until smooth.
- In a medium saucepan, cook the coconut milk, vanilla, salt, and arrowroot over low-medium heat for 10-12 minutes, or until thickened, stirring frequently. Do not boil. It will coat the back of a wooden spoon when it's ready.
- Mix half of the rhubarb compote (refrigerate the other half) into the gelato mixture and stir until fully combined. If you have an ice cream maker, cool, and follow the manufacturer's instructions. If not, pour into an 8x10 metal tray lined with parchment paper. Freeze for about four hours, stirring with a fork every hour, until frozen solid. After the first two hours, pour the remaining (cold) compote onto the gelato and swirl in with the fork.

- Let the gelato sit at room temperature for ten minutes before scooping and serving.

86. Rhubarb And Gin Sorbet With Rose Cream

Serving: Serves 8 | Prep: 0hours0mins | Cook: 0hours0mins | Ready in:

Ingredients

- For the rhubarb and gin sorbet:
- 8 ounces water
- 7 ounces granulated sugar
- 1 pound rhubarb, chopped
- 2 tablespoons fresh lime juice
- 2 tablespoons light corn syrup
- 2 tablespoons gin, plus a little more for serving
- For the rose cream:
- 4 ounces heavy cream
- 4 drops rose water, more to taste
- 2 teaspoons granulated sugar

Direction

- For the sorbet: Combine the sugar and water in a medium saucepan and heat on medium high, stirring occasionally until the sugar dissolves. Add in the rhubarb and simmer until the rhubarb is very tender and beginning to fall apart, about 10 minutes.
- Carefully transfer the mixture to a blender (or use an immersion blender) and blend until smooth. Add in the lime juice and corn syrup. Chill thoroughly.
- Just before churning, stir in the gin. Freeze and churn the chilled mixture in an ice cream machine, according to the manufacturer's instructions. Store in the freezer in an airtight container.
- For the rose cream: Whip the cream to soft peaks, then add in the sugar, followed by the rose water (one drop at a time) until desired flavor is reached.

- To serve: Top scoops of sorbet with a few drops of chilled gin and a spoonful of rose cream.

87. Rocky Road Ice Cream

Serving: Serves 4 people | Prep: 0hours10mins | Cook: 0hours10mins | Ready in:

Ingredients

- 1 (14 ounce) can sweetened condensed milk
- ½ cup unsweetened cocoa powder
- 2 cups heavy cream
- 1 cup light cream
- 1 tablespoon vanilla extract
- ½ cup chopped pecans
- 1 cup miniature marshmallows

Direction

- In a medium saucepan over low heat, cook and stir condensed milk and cocoa until smooth and slightly thickened, 5 minutes. Remove from heat, and allow to cool slightly. Stir in heavy cream, light cream, and vanilla. Refrigerate until cold.
- Pour mixture into the canister of an ice cream maker, and freeze according to manufacturer's directions. Stir in nuts and marshmallows halfway through the freezing process.
- Nutrition Facts
- Per Serving:
- 254 calories; protein 3.8g 8% DV; carbohydrates 19.3g 6% DV; fat 18.9g 29% DV; cholesterol 59mg 20% DV; sodium 53mg 2% DV.

88. Rosie Birkett's Foraged Fig Leaf And Blackberry Ripple Ice Cream

Serving: Serves 8 | Prep: | Cook: |Ready in:

Ingredients

- 300 milliliters double cream
- 300 milliliters whole milk
- 6 fig leaves
- 3 egg yolks
- 100 grams superfine sugar plus 1 tablespoon (or more), divided
- 1 pinch salt
- 200 grams blackberries

Direction

- NOTE: I always forget that when making ice cream, it's important to chill the custard overnight. So get started a day before you want to eat it!
- Heat the milk and cream with 50 grams of the sugar, until just boiling. Submerge the fig leaves in the mix and leave to infuse for about half an hour.
- In another bowl, whisk the egg yolks with 50 grams of the sugar and pinch of salt until pale and thick and ribbon-like. Strain the fig leaf infusion and drop a few drops of the yolk and sugar mix into the infused milk and cream. Stir, and then gently pour the infusion into the yolk mix, stirring steadily as you go, until it's all incorporated and you have a pale yellow mix. Wash out the pan you used to heat the milk and cream and return the mixture to the pan. Heat gently, stirring in a figure of eight movement until the custard is thick and leaves a clear trail on the wooden spoon.
- Remove from the heat and transfer to a bowl. Cover with a film of cling wrap directly on the custard's surface and refrigerate overnight.
- Make the blackberry purée by heating the blackberries with the remaining 1 tablespoon sugar in a non-stick pan. Cook until the blackberries collapse and release their juices.

Taste for sharpness and if they're particularly tart, add a dash more sugar. You want the purée to be sharp and sweet—perfectly balanced to cut through the sweet, creamy custard. Blitz in a food processor and strain out the seeds using a fine mesh sieve.

- The next day, churn the custard in an ice cream machine according to the manufacturer's instructions, until thick and creamy. About 5 minutes before the end of the churn, pour in some of the blackberry purée to achieve a ripple. It's up to you how much you add, but I like to keep some back so as to not overpower the fig leaf flavor. Transfer to a plastic container or ice cream tub and store in the freezer until needed.

89. Saffron Raspberry Swirl Ice Cream With Toasted Pistachios

Serving: Serves 6-8 | Prep: | Cook: |Ready in:

Ingredients

- Raspberry Syrup
- 1 pint Fresh Raspberries
- 1/2 cup Sugar
- 2 Strips of lemon peel (Use vegetable peeler)
- The Custard
- 5 Egg yolks (Large or extra large) at room temperature
- 3/4 cup Sugar
- 1 1/2 cups Heavy Cream
- 1 1/2 cups Whole milk
- Pinch of saffron (a little goes a long way)
- 1 1/2 teaspoons Vanilla Extract
- 1 tablespoon clear corn syrup
- 1/2 cup pistachios chopped and toasted

Direction

- Raspberry Syrup
- Add to saucepan the raspberries, sugar and lemon peel. Cook on med/high for about 10 minutes. Remove from heat and strain into a

bowl using a sieve you want to retain as much pulp as possible just leaving the seeds behind. Put in a jar or bowl covered with plastic wrap and refrigerate.

- The Custard
- Separate your eggs, place yolks in mixing bowl, add the sugar and beat with hand held mixer until pale and thick. In saucepan pour in cream and milk, add the pinch of saffron and heat to scalding do not bring to a boil. Drizzle half the heated cream and milk into the egg and sugar mixture whisking constantly you are tempering the eggs. Pour back into saucepan and cook on Medium heat stirring constantly with a wooden spoon. When it becomes thick turn spoon over and slide your finger down the back of the spoon, the custard is ready if the line you have drawn stays intact. Or you can use your thermometer and when the custard reaches a temperature of 165-170 it's done. Remove from heat.
- Pour into heatproof bowl or measuring cup add the vanilla and corn syrup and stir. Cover in plastic and refrigerate until cold must be 40 degrees or less. Chop the pistachios and either oven toast or pan toast them. I threw in a fry pan and toasted for about 2 minutes, stir frequently. Remove from heat transfer to a bowl to cool.
- When the custard is cold add to your ice cream maker and when it looks like soft serve ice cream add the chopped pistachios. To make the raspberry swirl you will need to do it in 3 stages. Place a third of the ice cream in your freezer container, generously drizzle raspberry syrup. Repeat for the other two layers. With a butter knife or a bamboo skewer carefully swirl around a couple of times careful not to overdo it you don't want it blended in with the custard. Place in freezer for approximately 4 hours so it's scoopable.

Serving: Makes 1 quart | Prep: | Cook: | Ready in:

Ingredients

- 1 1/2 cups blanched almonds (either coarsely chopped or slivered)
- 2 cups heavy cream
- 1 cup whole milk
- 2/3 cup sugar
- 2 tablespoons of your favorite honey (I like chestnut)
- 5 large egg yolks
- 1/2 teaspoon pure almond extract
- 1 tablespoon amaretto (optional)
- 1/4 teaspoon sea salt
- Optional mix-in: honeyed almond brittle (see recipe in Step 2 below)

Direction

- Preheat oven to 375 degrees F. On a baking sheet, spread the almonds in a single layer and toast them for 10 to 12 minutes, or until they're golden brown.
- (Optional) To make honeyed almond brittle: In a small skillet, toast 3/4 cup coarsely chopped (or sliced) almonds until they just start to color -- then add 3 T honey and a pinch of sea salt. Stir frequently over moderate heat until almonds are golden and coated with honey, about 4 minutes. Take off the heat, and using a spatula, spread in an even layer on a plate or cookie sheet lined with parchment and sprayed with non-stick spray, so the brittle doesn't stick. When cool, break into small pieces.
- To make the ice cream base: Whisk together the egg yolks and 1/3 cup sugar until the mixture is pale yellow.
- Meanwhile, in a large saucepan, whisk together heavy cream, whole milk, honey, and the remaining 1/3 cup sugar over medium-high heat until the sugar dissolves and small bubbles start to form. Stir in almonds, cover,

and remove from heat. Let sit for about 1 hour, or until infused with almond flavor. Taste and let sit longer if you want a stronger flavor. Strain it through a fine-mesh sieve into a bowl and discard the almonds (or save them for a snack).

- Put the milk/cream mixture back in the saucepan, bring it to a simmer, and then remove from heat. Add a little to the egg yolk mixture to warm it, starting with a few drops, then a slow and steady stream, about 1 cup total. Whisk constantly to prevent the egg yolks from curdling. Pour the egg yolk mixture back into the remaining hot milk/cream mixture; whisk together to combine.

- Return the custard to the stove and cook it over low heat, stirring constantly with a heatproof spatula, until it thickens enough to coat the spatula, about 7 to 10 minutes. If using an instant read thermometer, it should read around 170 degrees F (77 degrees C). Immediately take the saucepan off the heat, and strain the custard mixture through a fine-mesh sieve into a large bowl. Stir in the almond extract, salt, and amaretto (if using).

- Let the custard cool to room temperature, then refrigerate it at least 4 hours or overnight. (I sometimes accelerate this chilling process by putting the bowl in the freezer for 45 minutes or so – but set a timer so you don't forget about it. You want it to chill, not freeze!)

- To freeze the ice cream: Transfer chilled custard mixture to the bowl of your ice cream mixture, and freeze according to the manufacturer's instructions. If opting to mix-in honeyed almond brittle, fold into the freshly-churned ice cream. Transfer into an airtight container, and place a piece of plastic wrap directly over the surface to prevent crystals from forming. Cover and freeze until firm, about 2 hours. Ice cream should keep well for up to 2 weeks.

---

91. Secret Gelato

Serving: Makes about 3 cups | Prep: | Cook: | Ready in:

Ingredients

- 2 Avocados cut and frozen
- 2 Bananas cut and frozen
- 1/4 cup Coconut milk cold
- 1/4 cup Unsweetened cocoa
- 1/8 cup Agave Syrup
- 1 teaspoon Vanilla

Direction

- Ok going to have to try to simplify this. Put all the ingredients into the blender hit medium setting and blend till fluffy and smooth.
- Serve immediately and enjoy! If some is left over it can be froze but add coconut milk and agave to get consistency back

---

92. Strawberry Basil Tart With Avocado Ice Cream

Serving: Serves 8 | Prep: | Cook: | Ready in:

Ingredients

- Avocado Ice Cream
- 2 avocados, meat scooped out
- 1 lime, juiced
- 1 1/2 cups milk
- 1/2 cup sugar
- 1 cup heavy cream
- Strawberry Basil Tart
- 1 1/2 cups all purpose flour
- 2 tablespoons sugar
- 1 teaspoon cinnamon
- 1 teaspoon salt
- 5 ounces unsalted butter, chilled and cubed
- 1 egg yolk
- 2 tablespoons tequila blanco
- 2 pounds strawberries, de-stemmed and cut in half

- 1/2 cup sugar
- 1/2 cup Cointreau
- 1 orange, zest and juice
- 1 cup fresh basil leaves, chiffonade

Direction

- Avocado Ice Cream
- Puree avocados, lime juice, whole milk and sugar in a blender until very smooth in texture.
- Transfer to a medium mixing bowl and whisk in heavy cream until combined.
- Chill the mixture for a few hours in the refrigerator and then follow the instructions for your ice cream maker.
- Strawberry Basil Tart
- Mix together flour, sugar, cinnamon and salt in a large bowl until combined well. Using your hands, add butter and crumble into the flour (a food processor can also be used) until the crust mixture resembles a coarse meal.
- Add the egg yolk and the tequila, and mix together gently until dough is moist.
- Form dough into a flat disc, wrap in plastic and chill for at least 1 hour.
- Meanwhile mix together strawberries, sugar, Cointreau, orange zest and juice and the basil leaves. Let soak for at least an hour.
- Roll out dough on a floured surface until it forms a large circle about 16 inches in diameter. Ice cream will make it for you. Place rolled dough on a large, thick, greased cookie sheet with sides or, better yet, a large, greased cast iron pan.
- Place berries in a big pile in the center of the dough, reserving liquid.
- Fold dough up all around the pile of berries leaving a big hole at the top like a shallow volcano. Pour a little of the liquid in the top and reserve a little for the end.
- Bake in a preheated oven 375° for about 30 minutes or until crust is golden brown and crispy. Drizzle finished tart with the remainder of the juice from the berries.

93. Strawberry Frozen Yogurt Popsicles Dairy Free

Serving: Makes 9 | Prep: 2hours0mins | Cook: 0hours0mins | Ready in:

Ingredients

- 3 cups fresh or frozen strawberries
- 3/4 cup unsweetened plain dairy free yogurt
- 1 teaspoon vanilla extract
- 4 tablespoons maple syrup

Direction

- Add all of the ingredients into a high speed blender or food processor and blend until smooth and creamy. Adjust the sweetness to taste.
- Pour into pospsicle molds, place the lids and put in the freezer for 2 hours or until the yogurt is fully frozen. Just before serving run the popsicle mold under hot water for a few seconds to loosen the popsicle. Enjoy!

94. Strawberry Orange Sorbet

Serving: Serves 2 | Prep: | Cook: | Ready in:

Ingredients

- 2 sliced frozen bananas
- 1 cup frozen strawberries
- zest and juice of 1 orange
- 1/4 cup raw honey

Direction

- Put all of the ingredients in a blender and blend until smooth, pressing down with a tamper if necessary.
- Serve immediately

95. Strawberry Peach Sangria Pops

Serving: Makes 4 large popsicles | Prep: | Cook: |Ready in:

Ingredients

- 1 cup strawberries, diced
- 1 cup peaches, diced (skins and pits removed)
- 1/2 cup white grape juice
- 1/2 cup white wine (Riesling or Sauvignon Blanc would be nice, or perhaps a Rosé)
- Pinch cinnamon

Direction

- Place all of the ingredients in a blender and blend until smooth. Add a hint of superfine sugar as needed (I did not add sugar because my grape juice was plenty sweet).
- Pour into popsicle molds and freeze for 6 hours or overnight. If the popsicles are difficult to remove, run the tray under warm water and wiggle until the popsicles slide out easily. Enjoy!

96. Summer Corn Semifreddo With Rosemary Shortbread Crust And Blueberry Compote

Serving: Serves 10 to 12 | Prep: | Cook: |Ready in:

Ingredients

- For the summer corn semmifreddo:
- 2 medium ears corn, shucked
- 1 quart heavy cream
- 1/4 vanilla bean, split lengthwise and its seeds scraped and reserved
- 8 large egg yolks, at room temperature
- 3/4 cup sugar
- 1/2 teaspoon kosher salt
- 4 cups blueberries, stems removed, divided
- 1/2 cup plus 3 tablespoons sugar
- 1 tablespoon strained lemon juice
- Rosemary Shortbread, prepared, cooled, and crumbled (see below)
- For the rosemary shortbread:
- 2 1/2 teaspoons fresh rosemary, roughly chopped
- 1/2 teaspoon kosher salt
- 1 cup all-purpose flour
- 1/2 cup unsalted butter, softened to room temperature
- 1/3 cup sugar

Direction

- For the summer corn semmifreddo:
- Cut the kernels from corn cobs, reserving the cobs. In a large, heavy-bottomed saucepan, combine the kernels, cobs, cream, and the vanilla bean pod and seeds.
- Bring to a rolling boil and then remove from the heat. Transfer the mixture to a bowl, cover with plastic wrap, and chill for at least 12 hours and up to 2 days.
- In a medium stainless steel or glass bowl, whisk together the egg yolks, 1/2 cup sugar, and salt until smooth.
- Put the bowl over a pan of simmering water, making sure the bottom of the bowl does not touch the water. Whisk until the egg mixture is pale, thick and creamy, and an instant-read thermometer registers 160 degrees F, about 10 to 15 minutes. Put the bowl into a larger bowl of iced water to cool completely.
- Remove the cream mixture from the refrigerator and discard the cobs. Using an electric mixer, beat the cream until thick. Add the remaining 1/4 cup sugar and beat until the cream holds stiff peaks.
- Mix 1/4 of the cream into the cooled custard. Using a spatula, gently fold the remaining cream into the custard.
- Using 2 pieces of parchment paper, line a 9- by 13-inch cake pan, allowing the excess to hang over the ends and sides.
- Spoon the mixture into the prepared pan and cover with crumbled rosemary shortbread.

Fold the overhanging parchment paper, lightly pressing the shortbread into the custard and freeze for at least 8 hours or up to 3 days.

- Before serving, combine 2 cups blueberries with the sugar and lemon juice in a medium saucepan and bring to a simmer over medium-high heat, stirring frequently until the juices release, about 8 to 10 minutes.
- Increase the heat to high, bring the mixture to a boil, and cook, whisking frequently, until the compote is thickened, about 2 minutes. Transfer the compote to a clean bowl and gently fold in the remaining 2 cups uncooked berries.
- When ready to serve remove pan from freezer and let sit at room temperature for five minutes. Line a large baking sheet with parchment.
- Gently loosen the parchment and flip the pan onto the sheet lifting the pan away and removing the parchment layer. Cut into desired number of servings and top with blueberry compote.
- For the rosemary shortbread:
- Preheat the oven to 300° F. Combine the rosemary, salt, and flour in a medium bowl and set aside.
- Using a hand mixer, mix the butter and sugar in a large bowl until creamy. Gently fold in flour 1/4 cup at a time. (I use a plastic spatula until I've added all of the flour and then I finish bringing it together with my hands.)
- Gather the dough into a ball, cover in plastic wrap, and chill for 30 minutes to an hour. Roll the dough out into a rectangle of 1/2-inch thickness and cut into rectangles about 1/2-inch by 2-inch.
- Place the dough on a cold, ungreased baking sheet. Bake the shortbread for 30 minutes or until lightly browned.
- Remove the shortbread from the baking sheet and transfer to a rack to cool completely.

97. Sweet & Salty Banana Soft Serve With Roasted Almonds

Serving: Serves 4 | Prep: | Cook: | Ready in:

Ingredients

- Banana Soft-Serve
- 4 ripe bananas, frozen
- 2 tablespoons maple syrup
- 1/2 cup unsweetened almond milk
- 1 teaspoon vanilla paste (** or vanilla extract)
- (** optional add-ins: coconut, peanut butter, 1 scoop protein powder .. flavor of your choice)
- Roasted Almond Topping
- 1/4 cup almonds, finely chopped
- 2 teaspoons maple syrup
- 1/2 teaspoon coarse sea salt
- 1 teaspoon coconut oil (** or olive oil)

Direction

- Place bananas in the freezer for at least 3 hours. When you're ready to make the ice cream. Cut them into smaller pieces for easier blending
- In the meantime roast the almonds. In a small saucepan heat the oil over medium low for a minute or two. Add the chopped almonds & roast them for couple of minutes until they're starting to turn brown & are fragrant.
- In a bowl, combine the roasted almonds with 2 tsp syrup and salt.
- In a food processor, pulse frozen banana slices, almond milk, vanilla and remaining 2 tbsp. syrup, scraping down the sides as necessary, until mixture is the texture of soft-serve ice cream.
- Spoon into bowls. Sprinkle with almond mixture

98. Sweet Corn Ice Cream

Serving: Serves 4 | Prep: 0hours0mins | Cook: 0hours0mins | Ready in:

Ingredients

- 1 1/2 cups milk (whole or low-fat)
- 1 cup heavy cream
- 1/2 cup sugar
- 2 ears fresh sweet corn, shucked
- 4 egg yolks

Direction

- Cut the kernels off the corn cobs and reserve the cobs. Place kernels and cobs in a medium saucepan and add the milk, cream, and 1/4 cup of the sugar.
- Heat the milk mixture over medium heat until simmering, then remove from heat and let steep for 1 hour.
- Remove cobs from the milk mixture, and remove 1/2 cup of the corn kernels. Discard the cobs and reserve the kernels for later. Leave the rest of the corn kernels in the milk, and puree the mixture in a blender (or with an immersion blender) until smooth. Return the mixture to the saucepan and heat until simmering.
- Whisk the remaining 1/4 cup of sugar with the egg yolks in a large bowl. Slowly pour hot milk mixture into yolks, whisking constantly. Return mixture to saucepan and heat over low heat. Stir frequently, until mixture is thick and coats back of spoon. Immediately remove from heat and set a fine-mesh sieve over the large bowl that the egg yolks were in. Pour mixture over sieve, which will catch any egg that may have curdled.
- Allow ice cream batter to fully cool, then cover and put it in the fridge. Chill overnight, or at least 4 hours, then process in ice cream maker according to manufacturer's instructions.

99. Thai Iced Tea Ice Cream

Serving: Serves 6-8 | Prep: | Cook: |Ready in:

Ingredients

- 3 cups light cream
- 3 egg yolks
- 1 14 oz can of condensed milk
- 1 cup loose thai iced tea

Direction

- Gently heat cream mix with Thai tea over medium low heat until almost simmering. Turn off heat, and let steep for about 30 minutes.
- Strain the tea from the cream. Make custard by constantly whisking yolks into cream over gentle heat until bubbling and thickened.
- Stir in vanilla and condensed milk. Let chill, then freeze according to ice cream maker's instructions to yield about a quart.

100.   The Easiest Chocolate Frappe' With A Nutmeg Twist

Serving: Serves 1 | Prep: | Cook: |Ready in:

Ingredients

- 1 cup Good reduced fat milk
- 1 cup Chocolate ice cream
- Nutmeg

Direction

- Blend ice cream and milk together with a blender until very smooth. Pour in a cooled tall glass and grate a little nutmeg on top. Enjoy!

101.   Toffee Sauce With Beer

Serving: Makes 2 cups | Prep: | Cook: |Ready in:

Ingredients

- 1 1/2 cups (300 grams) dark or light brown sugar or light muscovado sugar
- 3 cups heavy cream
- 1 cup beer
- 1 1/2 teaspoons vanilla
- 1/8 teaspoon salt, or more to taste

Direction

- Combine the brown sugar, cream, and beer in a medium saucepan and heat to a simmer.
- Simmer, stirring frequently, until the sauce is reduced to 2 cups. Remove from heat and stir in the vanilla and salt.
- Let cool slightly, adjust salt and use right away, or cool and store until needed. Reheat to serve.

---

102.   Totally Luscious Raspberry Ice Cream

Serving: Serves 6 | Prep: | Cook: | Ready in:

Ingredients

- 17.8 ounces frozen raspberries
- 1/2 juice from half lemon
- 3/4 cup honey
- 4 egg yolks
- 3 tablespoons olive oil
- 13.5 coconut cream (placed in the fridge overnight and then drained of liquid)
- 1 teaspoon vanilla essence

Direction

- Place the defrosted raspberries and lemon juice into a pot and cook on low heat for 45 minutes or until reduced by half.
- Let cool to room temperature, strain through a sieve to remove the seeds, add the honey and combine.
- Mix the vanilla essence, egg yolks, oil and coconut cream until smooth. Then combine with the raspberries.

- Place into the fridge until cold and then into your ice cream maker as per the manufacturer's instructions.
- Once churned, place the ice cream into a shallow airtight dish in the freezer for two hours before serving.

---

103.   Vegan Cherry Ice Cream

Serving: Makes 1 quart | Prep: | Cook: | Ready in:

Ingredients

- 14 ounces Coconut milk (1 can full fat)
- 2 cups Dark sweet cherries
- 2 teaspoons Vanilla
- 1 squeeze Fresh lemon juice
- 1 pinch Salt
- Stevia, to taste
- 2 tablespoons Rum, brandy, or similar liquor

Direction

- Use very ripe, fresh, deeply colored cherries. Wash, pit, and remove stems and pack lightly into a measuring cup until you have 2 cups.
- Put all ingredients except stevia into a blender and process until smooth.
- Add stevia to taste. The amount will vary depending on the brand and age of the stevia. Use plain white powder (a brand with fillers is acceptable if you can't find plain but do not use green). Add small amounts, blend, and taste. The liquid will become more and sweeter until it is just right. At this point, add just a touch more so that it is slightly oversweet. The cold will tone it down and bring it back to perfection. Alternate recipe: Use another sweetener of your choice instead of stevia.
- Add the liquor (optional but will help the texture, as well as the taste). Pulse the blender briefly to mix.

- Pour the mixture into an ice cream machine and freeze according to the manufacturer's directions.

104. Vegan Coconut Sweetcorn Ice Cream

Serving: Makes 1 quart | Prep: | Cook: | Ready in:

Ingredients

- 13.5 cups Coconut Milk, full fat
- 14 ounces Coconut Cream, full fat
- 1/8 cup Agave syrup
- 1/2 cup Sugar in the Raw
- 2 ears Sweetcorn, cut off the husk
- 1 Vanilla Bean, split
- 1/2 teaspoon Sea Salt

Direction

- In a saucepan over medium heat, combine the coconut milk, cream, corn (and husks) and vanilla. Stir every ten minutes for 30 minutes.
- Stir in salt, syrup and sugar and let it sit, covered for an hour
- Cover the liquid mixture with a lid or plastic wrap and refrigerate until very cold, for about 3-4 hours
- Transfer into freezer until firm enough to scoop, about 6 hours.

105. Vegan/Gluten Free DQ Copycat Ice Cream Cake

Serving: Makes 1 cake | Prep: | Cook: | Ready in:

Ingredients

- FUDGE/COOKIE LAYER
- 3 chia eggs (3 tbsp chia seeds mixed with 9 tbsp water)
- 1 cup cane sugar
- 1/2 cup powdered peanut butter
- 1/2 cup cocoa powder
- 4 tablespoons water
- Chocolate/Vanilla Ice Cream Layer
- 9 bananas (sliced and frozen)
- 2 tablespoons maple syrup
- 1/4 cup cocoa powder

Direction

- FUDGE/COOKIE LAYER
- Preheat oven to 350 F
- Line the bottom of a 9" cake pan with parchment paper
- In a large mixing bowl create the chia eggs (combine 3 tbsp. chia seeds and 9 tbsp. water and let sit 5 minutes)
- Add the sugar, powered peanut butter, cocoa powder, and 4 tbsp. water to chia eggs. Whisk to combine.
- Pour 2/3 of the mixture in the parchment lined cake pan
- Place in freezer (This layer must freeze at least 3 hours before layering in ice cream!)
- Line baking sheet with silicon baking mat or parchment paper
- Pour remaining fudge mixture on baking sheet and spread in a thin even layer about 1/8" thick
- Bake 15-20 min or until no longer tacky (It will become really dull in color. We're looking for crunchy not burnt so keep an eye on it!)
- Move silicon mat to a wire rack to cool
- After completely cool break into pieces and put into a Ziploc bag, crush up with a mallet/wooden spoon/rolling pin into small pieces
- Set aside
- Chocolate/Vanilla Ice Cream Layer
- Line bottom of a spring form pan with parchment paper
- Add 4 1/2 frozen bananas, 1 tbsp. maple syrup, and 1/4 cup cocoa powder to a food processor and pulse until smooth
- Pour chocolate mixture into pan and smooth into an even layer

- Freeze at least 30 minutes before proceeding!
- Add 4 1/2 frozen bananas and 1 tbsp. maple syrup to a food processor and pulse until smooth
- Take spring form pan and cake pan from freezer
- Remove fudge layer from cake pan (this defrosts very quickly and is very sticky! handle carefully) flip upside down into spring form and slowly peel off the parchment
- Take cookie crumbles and sprinkle over top of fudge layer
- Pour vanilla ice cream mixture on top and smooth into an even layer
- Freeze overnight (At least! I made mine 2 days ahead to make sure it was very solid all the way through.)
- When you're ready to unveil your cake take a dish towel and dampen it with warm water. Wrap the dish towel around the spring form pan for about 30 seconds this helps the cake release from the sides of the pan. Say a prayer and open the spring. Remove cake from pan. Hold the cake and peel the parchment from the bottom and place on serving platter.

---

106.   Vietnamese Iced Coffee Ice Box Cake

Serving: Serves 8 | Prep: 1hours30mins | Cook: 12hours0mins | Ready in:

Ingredients

- Coffee Fudge
- 2 ounces dark chocolate (72% or darker), chopped
- 6 tablespoons strong coffee (cold brew or espresso for a stronger coffee flavor)
- 4 tablespoons unsweetened cocoa powder
- 1 pinch kosher salt
- 1/4 cup heavy cream
- 4 tablespoons granulated sugar
- 4 tablespoons light corn syrup

- Condensed Milk Cream & Other Ice Box Cake Ingredients
- 2 1/2 cups heavy cream, chilled
- 2 tablespoons vanilla extract
- 1/3 cup powdered sugar
- 1 pinch kosher salt
- 1/2 cup sweetened condensed milk
- 1 packet graham crackers (1 box to be safe)
- 2 ounces dark chocolate (72% or darker), chopped

Direction

- Make the coffee fudge by first combining 6 tbsp. of strong coffee, 4 tbsp. of unsweetened cocoa powder, 1 pinch of kosher salt and 2 oz. of dark chocolate (roughly chopped) in a medium size bowl. Whisk together vigorously then set aside.
- In a saucepan over medium-high heat, combine 1/2 cup of heavy cream, 4 tbsp. of granulated sugar and 4 tbsp. of light corn syrup. Stir frequently to ensure the sugar has melted and that the cream does not burn. Once the mixture comes to a boil (bubbles break across the surface), pour immediately over the coffee / chocolate mixture and let sit for a full minute. Once the minute has passed, whisk together the combined mixture until smooth (3-5 minutes).
- Let chocolate coffee mixture cool (which will look more like chocolate milk than fudge) to room temperature before placing in the fridge for 45 minutes to 1 hour. Once properly cooled, the combined mixture will thicken to a fudge consistency.
- While the fudge cools, make the condensed milk cream. In a stand mixer bowl that has been chilled in the freezer for 10-15 minutes, combine 2 1/2 cups of chilled heavy cream and 2 tbsp. of vanilla extract. Using the whisk attachment, whisk on the lowest speed for 1-2 minutes before increasing the speed up to medium. Whisk until the mixture has reached soft peaks.
- Once the mixture has reached soft peak consistency, add in 1/3 cup of powdered

sugar and the pinch of kosher salt. Mix on medium speed until well incorporated.

- Take the bowl off the stand mixer and using a silicone spatula, slowly incorporate the condensed milk into the cream by drizzling 1/4 cup of condensed milk slowly before folding it gently into the mixture. This will essentially swirl condensed milk throughout the cream. Set aside in the refrigerator until ready to use.
- To assemble the cake once the fudge and condensed milk cream are ready, line an 8.5" by 4.5" loaf pan with plastic wrap both horizontally and vertically to allow easy removal of the cake once completed (usually 3-4 layers to be safe). Allow enough overhang over the sides so that the cake can be easily lifted out and wrapped with excess plastic wrap.
- On the bottom of the loaf pan, layer one single layer of graham crackers, making sure the loaf pan is completely filled (cutting pieces of graham crackers to fill any spots).
- Next, spread a layer of coffee fudge over the graham crackers. Then, spread a layer of condensed milk cream (reserve at least 1 cup of whipped cream for serving, keep in fridge until needed). Drizzle a few tbsp. of the remaining condensed milk and then top with chocolate shavings. Continue to alternate layers starting with the graham crackers, coffee fudge, condensed milk cream, condensed milk drizzle and chocolate shavings until you've reached the top of the loaf pan.
- Wrap tightly in plastic wrap and refrigerate overnight or at least 12 hours. Once you're ready to serve, unwrap the icebox cake and flip over onto a serving platter. Top the cake with the remaining whipped cream and top with chocolate shavings.

Serving: Serves 8 | Prep: | Cook: |Ready in:

Ingredients

- Main Ingredients
- 1/2 pound pitted plums, roughly chopped
- 3/4 cup plus a tablespoon sugar, divided, plus more as needed
- 2 1/2 cups cashew cream (recipe follows)
- 1/4 cup light corn syrup
- 2 tablespoons white miso paste
- Cashew Cream
- 1 3/4 cups raw unsalted cashews ("raw" as in not roasted, etc. Unless you want to shell out serious dough for truly raw cashews, all of them have been treated to remove the cashew's toxic shell)
- Filtered water to cover, for soaking
- 1 1/2 cups filtered water

Direction

- Main Ingredients
- Toss plums with a tablespoon (or more, depending on the sweetness of your plums) sugar in saucepan and cook, over medium heat, until bubbling and saucy, about 15 minutes. Puree briefly in blender or food processor (you want it to be a little chunky still, so don't make plum soup).
- Meanwhile, bring the cashew milk, remaining 3/4 cup sugar and corn syrup to a simmer in saucepan over medium heat. Remove from heat and set aside.
- Place cashew milk mixture and miso in a blender. Process until smooth.
- Cover and chill both mixtures in refrigerator for 2-3 hours or overnight.
- Process ice cream as per manufacturer's instructions. Once ice cream is done, spoon some of the plum mixture into your storage container; scoop in some of your cashew ice cream. Alternate scoops of plum mixture and ice cream; you may have more plum mixture

than needed, reserve any excess for another use. Cover and freeze for 2-3 hours. Let sit 15 minutes before serving.
- Cashew Cream
- Soak cashews in filtered water for 2-3 hours or overnight. Drain and rinse.
- Place the soaked cashews and measured filtered water in blender; process until smooth (taking breaks to scrape down the sides and blend again if you have a less-than-high-powered blender like mine).

108. Zucchini Bread Ice Cream

Serving: Makes 2 quarts | Prep: | Cook: | Ready in:

Ingredients

- 4 tablespoons butter
- 2 large zucchini, grated (about 1 pound)
- 3 cups heavy cream
- 1/2 cup whole milk
- 1/4 teaspoon ground cinnamon
- 1/4 teaspoon ground clove
- 1/4 teaspoon ground coriander
- 1/4 teaspoon freshly grated nutmeg
- 1/4 teaspoon ground black pepper
- 8 large egg yolks
- 3/4 cup sugar
- 1/2 cup beer, IPA
- 1/2 teaspoon vanilla
- 1 1/2 teaspoons kosher salt

Direction

- Melt the butter in a 2 quart sauce pot. Sweat the zucchini and the salt to nearly au sec. It will look like a mushy paste. Take care not to burn as the mixture reduces.
- Transfer to a blender with the spices and whole milk. Blend until smooth. Return to the pan along with the heavy cream. Bring to just below a simmer.

- Whisk the egg yolks with the sugar until pale in color. Add 1/2 cup of the hot zucchini mix, whisking rapidly to incorporate. Add the yolk mixture back into the pot, whisking constantly.
- Cook over med-low heat, stirring frequently, until mixture coats the back of a spoon. Strain the ice cream base through a fine-meshed sieve into a stainless steel bowl and chill over an ice bath. Stir in the beer and vanilla. Churn in an ice cream maker.

109. Frozen Espresso Yogurt With Caramelized Honey Bourbon Oranges

Serving: Serves 2 | Prep: | Cook: | Ready in:

Ingredients

- yogurt "ice cream"
- 1 cup greek yogurt plain, I used the greek gods
- 1 tablespoon espresso powder or instant coffee, decaf
- orange topping
- 1 large orange, zest, fruit and juice
- 4 tablespoons honey bourbon
- 1/8 cup sugar
- 1/8 cup water

Direction

- Mix yogurt and espresso together in bowl, cover with plastic wrap and freeze 1 hour, stir, freeze 1/2 hour, stir, freeze 1/2 hour
- Zest orange, cut off rind, do not peel, you want to cut off all the pith and skin, then cut out fruit from between skin sections. Squeeze rest of fruit to get out all the juices, add bourbon to juice and fruit.
- 15 minutes before yogurt is ready, put zest and juice/bourbon (not the fruit) in a sauce pan with sugar and water. Stir till sugar is

mostly dissolved and heat over medium heat, do not stir again. 5 minutes

- Add remaining fruit to sauce and continue to cook, it may be a low boil, until sauce thickens to a caramel consistency.
- Stir yogurt one last time and scoop into 2 small bowls, pour sauce over and enjoy!

- Peel and cube watermelon, catching juices. A god way to do this is to cut on a board that fits inside a rimmed cookie sheet.
- Cut tomatoes, catching juices
- Blend all the ingredients together, and then send through a food mill into a bowl.
- If not already cold, chill the mixture overnight. Freeze in a counter top ice cream maker according to manufacturer's directions, pack gently into a quart container. This is icy, bur should retain it's scoop-ability if not packed too densely

110.   Peachy Frosé

Serving: Serves 2 to 4 | Prep: | Cook: | Ready in:

Ingredients

- 16 ounces frozen peaches
- 750 milliliters good quality rosé
- honey (optional)
- fresh peach slices, for garnish

Direction

- Fill a blender with the peaches and the rose and blend until smooth and slushy. Add a dash of honey if you like it sweeter. Pour into glasses and serve with a fresh peach slice.

111.   Watermelon And Tomato Gazpacho Sorbet

Serving: Makes 1 quart | Prep: | Cook: | Ready in:

Ingredients

- 1 small watermelon
- 2-3 sweet tomatoes
- 1/8 cup good fruity olive oil
- 3/4 cup sugar
- 1 dash salt

Direction

Index

Conclusion

Thank you again for downloading this book!

I hope you enjoyed reading about my book!

If you enjoyed this book, please take the time to share your thoughts and post a review on Amazon. It'd be greatly appreciated!

Write me an honest review about the book – I truly value your opinion and thoughts and I will incorporate them into my next book, which is already underway.

Thank you!

If you have any questions, **feel free to contact at:** *author@syruprecipes.com*

Nancy Reed

syruprecipes.com

Printed in Great Britain
by Amazon

73046362R00038